The Independent Walker's Guide to Italy

Other titles in the series

The Independent Walker's Guide to France
The Independent Walker's Guide to Great Britain
The Independent Walker's Guide to Ireland

The Independent Walker's Guide to Italy

by Frank Booth

35 Breathtaking Walks
in Italy's Captivating Landscape

INTERLINK BOOKS
NEW YORK

First published in 1998 by

INTERLINK BOOKS
An imprint of Interlink Publishing Group, Inc.
99 Seventh Avenue
Brooklyn, New York 11215

Library of Congress Cataloging-in-Publication Data

Booth, Frank W., 1951–
The independent walker's guide to Italy / by Frank Booth.
p. cm.—(The independent walker series)
"35 breathtaking walks in Italy's captivating landscape."
ISBN 1-56656-210-4 (alk. paper)
1. Italy—Guidebooks. 2. Walking—Italy—Guidebooks. I. Title.
II. Series
DG416.B66 1998
914.504'929—dc20 96-38970
CIP

Printed and bound in Canada
10 9 8 7 6 5 4 3 2

Contents

Part Two: 35 Great Walks

Contents

Introduction

Although this is a walkers' guide, it is also about escaping and avoiding the DROPS. The DROPS are not a communicable disease. They are something far more insidious: the DREADED OTHER PEOPLE who are always in your way, going where you want to go when you want to go. You have seen them everywhere—in long lines at the bank, at the supermarket with bounteous baskets standing six deep in front of you, and in disabled vehicles blocking your path during interminable rush-hour traffic. Great multitudes of DROPS are waiting for you in Italy.

Seldom will you see a single DROP (perhaps this word can only be used in the plural; a single individual may not qualify for DROPhood). They tend to cluster in large numbers around people who are trying to avoid them. Like stampeding cattle, they destroy everything in their path. International publications are currently reporting the results of their rampaging: as *Newsweek* put it in July 1992, "These days it is tough to find a vacation spot that doesn't in some way resemble a shopping mall, a garbage dump, or a traffic jam."

Even with this book in hand, you will not always be able to completely avoid the DROPS, but you will have a strategy to retain your independence and sanity. For example, if you are sojourning in Rome, you will want to visit Hadrian's Villa at Tivoli where you will be shoulder to shoulder with numerous DROPS; however, when you leave Tivoli do not allow yourself to be herded into a bus or train for an express commute back to Rome. Take the quick, six-mile walk from the lovely hill town of San Polo dei Cavalieri back to Tivoli along a superb cliff-side path with astounding views of lovely hills and valleys all the way into Tivoli. You will probably spend less time along the trail than you did in lines at Hadrian's Villa, and you will see none of the DROPS whose elbows you encountered while you toured that cavernous site. You can repeat this scenario at many of the most renowned tourist sites in Italy. You will see the "must-sees," but you will also get way off the beaten path for a glimpse of the real Italy that is known only to the independent walker.

This book shows you how to walk between and around sites that are endlessly written about in ordinary guides. The trails described in this book will take you to many of Italy's most famous monuments and also to a variety of lesser known but equally interesting areas. The one or two hours on foot from tourist centers is a world away from the ordinary tourist's view of Italy. You will enter another dimension and go one step (actually a lot of steps) beyond into the outer limits of an ordinary tour of Italy. You will see Italians going about their daily lives on farms, in villages, and along roads too remote to appear or most maps. Local cows, horses, sheep, chicken, and dogs will often be present to greet you. Explore Italy as a traveller, not a tourist, and truly see all of Italy through the back door.

This book is organized into two sections. The first part, Hitting the Trail, provides general information on travel to Italy and what to expect when you arrive: from how to use public transportation and driving tips to information about hotels and restaurants. And of course it also supplies you with all the information you need to become a successful hiker in Italy. The second section contains practical information about thirty-five great walks, including distance, time duration, and a general description of the trail and local sights. Each walk description also has an accompanying set of trail notes and maps that will alert you to possible problems and confusion along the route, and help you plot your course through undiscovered Italy.

Walking as Opposed to Other Forms of Travel

Why not rent a car or take a train or a bus or even pedal a bicycle? Why walk? There are faster ways of getting around, and if you go faster, you can see more. I understand this mentality and have been on some breathtaking auto tours of Europe, hurtling down expressways from sight to sight at one hundred miles per hour while German sedans pass at warp speed. If driving quickly between famous sites will be the extent of your vacation, stay home, rent a travel video about Italy, and save money.

Although I recommend travel by car, you should also take the time for frequent walks. When you walk, you create unique memories, avoid the DROPS, and seldom see any mechanized form of transportation. All of these are luxuries afforded to few twentieth-century travellers.

Trains and buses in Italy are generally very good, and you will want to use these modes of transportation as an aid to your walking. However, I would not recommend spending valuable vacation time riding around on crowded public transportation, particularly during the summer months when the DROPS assemble en masse. When you take a train or bus, you often miss the most important part of your trip—the trail or what lies between your destinations. There are no surprises on public transportation, and you will probably have numerous DROPS and dirty windows separating you from what you came to see: Italy.

Some people extol the virtues of bicycling in Europe. Yes, you will get some exercise, and you will see some interesting monuments. You will not, however, get far off the beaten path; bicycles go where cars go—where everyone else goes. The roads that cyclists pedal are less frequented by motorized vehicles but by no means untravelled. Many of these roads are very narrow, almost too narrow for two cars and too narrow for two cars and a bicycle. The traffic in Italy almost always goes at a breakneck pace and there is very little reverence for cyclists. Do not count on drivers watching out for you; you are definitely on your own. Furthermore, European cars are notorious for their choking emissions and high-decibel noise. On a trail, you will encounter none of these difficulties.

The Independent Walker

This book is designed to help you, an independent traveller, plan a walking tour of Italy. There is no single way of walking in Italy, and whether you are relying on your thumb for locomotion and sleeping in an army-surplus pup tent or leasing a Mercedes to shuttle yourself between multi-starred luxury hotels, you will find this book to be worth more than you paid for it.

All of the walks have been selected based on the following criteria: the walk itself is of great visual delight; the trail is near a noteworthy tourist site or in an area of great natural beauty; there is easy access to public transportation. Another unique feature of this book is that all of the walks are linear (except two which are in areas where absolutely no motorized vehicles are allowed); you will not find yourself walking around in circles (i.e., getting nowhere). Linear walks are interesting throughout their entire length, whereas circular walks, which you will find in other walking guides, usually include a less-than-attractive or repetitious return to the starting point. Linear walks also impart a feeling of accomplishment in having arrived at a town or city in the traditional way of our ancestors, on foot. At Rome, for example, you will trace the path of the ancient Appian Way where you will marvel at millenia-old funeral monuments and stop at ancient Christian catacombs before passing through a seventeen-hundred-year-old Roman gate and arriving at the Roman Forum, seeing many of the same sights and monuments that would have delighted an ancient Roman. Similar experiences await you throughout Italy. You can use a car and public transportation or, if you do not rent a car, use only public transportation to reach starting and ending points. Specific directions are included in the final section for each walk.

In order to plan a remarkable tour of Italy, consult the map on page 6, and look at the suggested itineraries listed below. For travellers with time to burn, there is a comprehensive itinerary, the Grand Tour, which combines all of the greatest sites with a collection of Italy's finest walks. The Grand Tour is peerless as a vehicle for an in-depth discovery of Italy.

There are also three regional itineraries: The North: Lakes, Mountains, and Beaches; Rome, Tuscany, Umbria, and the Adriatic Coast; and Rome, the South, and Sicily. Another unique feature of this book is the inclusion of ten thematic tours: Ancient Ruins; Great Castles and Walls; Famous Cathedrals, Churches, and Abbeys; Fabulous Forests; High Hills and Massive Mountains; Captivating Coasts and Beaches; Inland Waterways; Great Art Centers; Must-See Itinerary: All the Greatest Sights; and Author's Favorite Walks.

Although there is a remarkable diversity of tours available to select from, do not consider this to be a straightjacket. Feel free to construct your own itinerary or combine two or more of the suggested itineraries. In order to determine which particular walks are most attractive for you, inspect the Walks-at-a-Glance section on pages 21–40, which provides capsule summaries of each adventure.

Itineraries

The following diverse itineraries are suggested, but feel free to construct your own via consultation with the maps and walk summaries.

The Grand Tour

For the finest tour available in all of Italy, complete all of the walks in the order presented (1–35) or in the sequence presented in the regional itineraries. An ambitious, fast driving traveller could do them all in about seven weeks with a few days left over for a stay in Rome. For a less frenetic tour, budget about eight or nine weeks. For more details, consult the three regional itineraries.

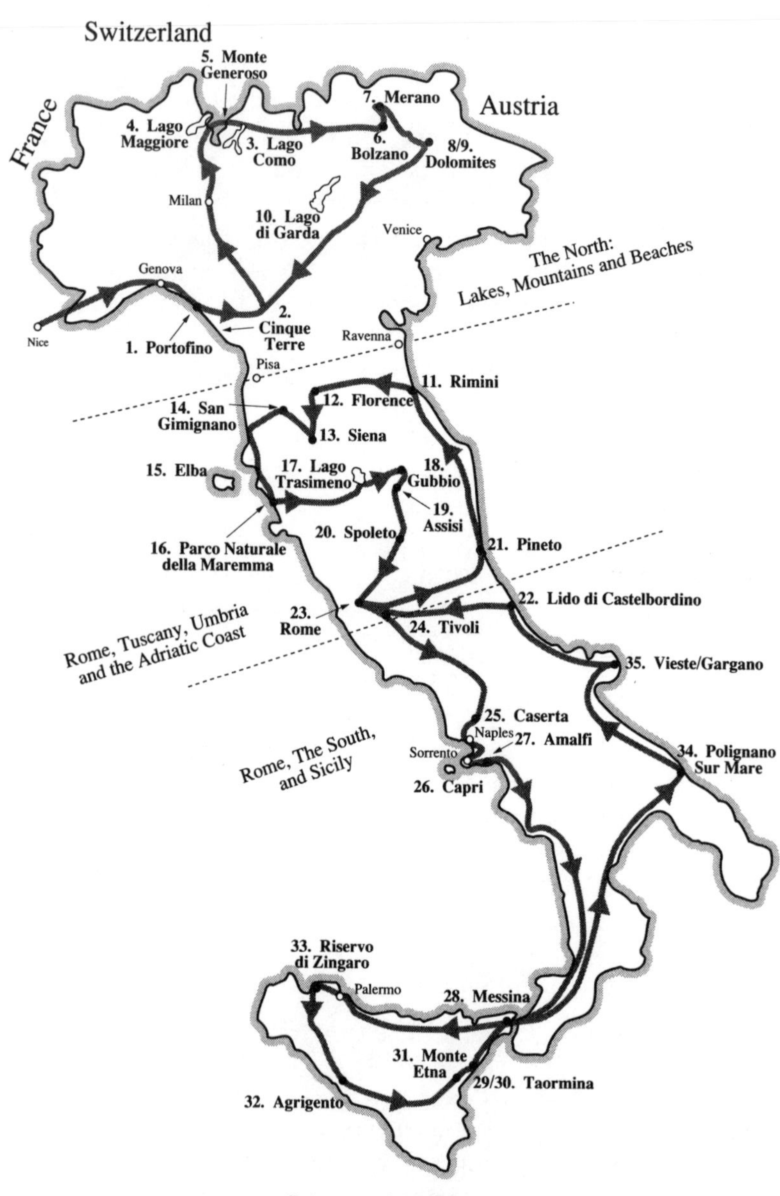

Itineraries Map

Regional Itineraries

The itineraries are given here in their most compressed form. If you are not on a tight schedule, feel free to intersperse your walks with free days to explore each region in more depth or simply to relax. Also, on one-night stops you may not arrive in time to make a required public transportation rendezvous, necessitating an extra day in town; or you may not feel like getting out of your car and going immediately on a walk. Be judicious with available time, and do not push yourself too hard. Remember, you are on vacation. On the other hand, it usually is possible for tireless travellers to adhere to the suggested itineraries and enjoy the fast-paced succession of sites and walks. The suggested travel routes are simply the fastest (remember, routes designated "A" or "*autostrada*" are toll roads, while all other roads are free) or most direct. Please ignore them, if you have the time, and create a more interesting route along Italy's beautiful back roads. These itineraries, which take you to a variety of off-the-beaten-path locations, are sometimes more difficult via public transportation and may involve convoluted routing in order to reach some destinations. However, for the patient traveller it is possible to arrive at all of the destinations, and I have indicated whether it is possible to reach a destination by train or if a train/bus combination is required. You can get detailed information on connections at most train stations, or you can consult *Let's Go: Italy* or the Berkeley Guide's *Italy on the Loose* for reliable public transportation information. Also, for less than $3 (£2) each, you can purchase the complete train schedules for Nord (north), Centro (central), and Sud (south) Italy. Published under the general title *Nuovo Grippaudo Orario,* these schedules can be purchased at bookstores and *edicoli* (street vendors that specialize in magazines) throughout Italy, especially those near train stations. Finally, the suggestions about where to stay can easily be altered to suit your needs; however, they are generally the most attractive alternative in a given area. I have included some specific lodging recommendations, but the tourist office, a quick ride around town, or a comprehensive guidebook that specializes in lodging will provide you with a more in-depth overview of the local lodging scene. Rooms are seldom difficult to find in Italy, especially if you are in a car. However, if you are relying on public transportation, you may wish to consult a comprehensive guide book and reserve hotel rooms in advance.

1. *The North: Lakes, Mountains, and Beaches*

Italy's unparalleled natural beauty is the focus of this itinerary, where ubiquitous, ethereal panoramas will have you basking in a state of permanent astonishment. It is best to fly into Milan for this itinerary or to Nice in France where rental cars are much less expensive, and the scenic drive to the Italian border is less than 45 minutes.

Nights 1–3: Rapallo (Walks 1 and 2)

From Nice in France, drive east to the Italian border along A8. Continue in Italy along the autostrada A10 which follows the coast past Genoa where you continue on A12 until you reach Rapallo (150 miles/2½ hours); or by train, first to Genoa where you will change to a train healing for La Spezia. From Milan, take A7 to Genoa and then A12 to Rapallo (110 miles/2 hours); or by train, switching at Genoa. Rapallo is a very attractive beach resort with numerous lodgings (try the moderately priced Hotel Stella at 10 Via Aurelia Ponente, tel. 0185 50 367, which has a garage in a town where parking is at a premium) and dining opportunities. Beyond a local castle, there are no important sights. However, you may sun and swim in style at Rapallo, and you may conveniently take the boat to Portofino and the train to Cinque Terre from here. If you prefer, any of the other local resort towns will prove to be adequate for Walks 1 and 2. Relax and roam along the beach front on day 1 while completing Walk 1 (San Fruttuoso to Portofino) and Walk 2 (Vernazza to Riomaggiore) on the following two days.

Nights 4–6: Lakes (Walks 3–5)

You could stay anywhere in Italy's Lake District and be surrounded by some of the finest natural beauty in the world. Como, on the shores of Lake Como, is particularly attractive and provides a convenient base of operations for Lake District exploration. To reach Como from Rapallo (140 miles/2½ hours), drive along A12 to Genoa, then A7 to Milan, and finally A9 to Como; or by train via Genoa and Milan. Rooms can be difficult to find during the summer, but you can always cruise in search of a room around the lake through the small towns that cling to its shores. The Hotel Ristorante Glavjc (tel. 031 41 93 00), located in Torno just north of Como, is beautifully situated along the lake shore and offers a restaurant and rooms with stunning views. You will have time to complete Walk 3 (Brunate to Como) on the first day and Walk 4 (Cannero to Cannobio; from Como via route N2 or by train to Capolago on the eastern shore of Lake Lugano) and Walk 5 (Vetta to Bellavista or Melano; by car from Como to Luino via Varese on routes 342, 233, and 394; or by train via Bellinzona) on the subsequent two days.

Nights 7–10: Mountains (Walks 6–9)

Beautiful Bolzano, conveniently situated near the *autostrada,* is an excellent base for exploring the hills and mountains of northern Italy. From Como the ride to Bolzano is all super highway (200 miles/3½ hours) along A9, A4, and A22; or Bolzano can be reached by train, switching at Milan. Although Bolzano can be crowded, the tourist office is quite helpful and can almost always find rooms. Spend your first day here relaxing and enjoying the lofty ambience. On the subsequent three days, complete Walks 6 (Oberbozen to Bolzano), 7 (Algund to Merano; by car, route 38; or by train), and 8/9 (both based at St. Christina; by car, A22 to route 242; or by bus) which you may combine. Alternately, you may wish to use Merano, one of the most beautiful cities I have ever seen, as a base for Walks 6 and 7. To complete Walks 8 and 9 find lodging in the mountainous Selva/Wolkenstein area.

Night 11: Lago di Garda (Walk 10)

Lago di Garda, largest and least touristed of the Italian lakes, is easily reached by car from Bolzano (85 miles/2 hours: A22 south to Rovereto Sud/Lago di Garda Nord exit, route 240 west to Torbole, route 249 south to Marniga or Castelletto) but more difficult by public transportation (trains to Verona and Peschiera, then bus to Marniga or Castelletto). Spend the night along the shores in Marniga, Castelletto, or one of the other numerous towns that hug the coast and complete Walk 10 (Marniga to Castelletto). Return to Milan (110 miles/2½ hours) or Nice (310 miles/6 hours).

2. *Rome, Tuscany, Umbria, and the Adriatic Coast*

Perfect for first-time travellers to Italy, this itinerary includes many of the most popular tourist sights and can be completed expeditiously with a minimum of driving. You will enjoy a stunning combination of sandy beaches, Roman ruins, medieval tranquillity, and Renaissance culture as you traverse through some of Italy's most alluring countryside. This tour proposes an unbeatable combination of urban sophistication and rural solitude.

Nights 1–3: Pineto, Silvi Marina, or Atri (Walks 21 and 22)

Drive from Rome straight to the Adriatic Sea (145 miles/3½ hours: A24, A25 east to Pescara, A14 north; or by train via Pescara). Stay at one of the numerous hotels in Pineto or Silvi Marina. If you prefer a quieter, hill-town atmosphere, drive to lovely Atri about 10 miles inland from Pineto and stay at the most attractive Hotel du Parc (tel. 085 870 260). Relax, swim, and stroll about on the first day, and complete Walk 21 (Silvi Marina to Pineto) on day 2. On the third day, the more adventurous will cruise down the coast to Lido di Casalbordino to complete Walk 22.

Night 4: Rimini (Walk 11)

From Pineto, drive north (A14: 145 miles/2½ hours; or by the coastal train) to Rimini where there are more hotels than grains of sand on the beach. Enjoy the exotic ambience and complete Walk 11. From here, you may wish to drive north for a couple of days in order to visit Ravenna and Venice. Both of these world-class tourist destinations merit a detailed visit, but there are no suitable walks in the vicinity of either city.

Nights 5–6: Florence (Walk 12)

Florence is one of the great cultural centers of the world, and you could easily extend your visit by several days or even weeks. Also, it is possible to complete Walks 13 (Siena) and 14 (San Gimignano) as a day trip. From Rimini, you can take a series of scenic back roads over enchanting hill country, but it will take you an eternity. If you are in a hurry, cruise quickly along the *autostrada* (A14 north to Bologna, A1 south to A11 east to Florence: 135 miles/2½ hours; or by train via Bologna). The easiest place to book one of the numerous rooms in Florence is at the Consorzia ITA in the train station. Parking is difficult in Florence, and you may have to pay to garage your vehicle. Scratch the surface of Florence's abundant tourist sights on the first day, and then complete Walk 12 on day two.

Night 7: Siena (Walk 13)

Siena, another stunning city worthy of more than a single day's inspection, can be quickly reached by automobile (45 miles/1 hour) or by train. Siena can also be visited as a day trip from Florence. Siena has numerous hotel rooms (but few budget accommodations) which can be booked at the Siena Hotels Promotion office near the bus station. Take Walk 13 early and enjoy the rest of the day in this lovely Renaissance city.

Night 8: San Gimignano (Walk 14)

The towers of San Gimignano are not far (about 40 miles) from Siena or Florence. Trains or buses necessitate a transfer to a local bus at Poggibonsi. Book a room at the tourist office; take Walk 14; and stroll about this treasure of a town while contemplating long-ago times.

Nights 9–10: Piombino (Walks 15 and 16)

Piombino exists as a port town and gateway to elegant Elba (minor road from San Gimignano in the direction of Volterra to route 68 then to E80 just before Cecina, where you continue south to Piombino; or by train from Poggibonsi). It is not a beautiful town, but it does have a certain real-Italy sort of charm. In any case, you will not be in town long, because your two days here will be consumed by outstanding excursions. There are not a lot of rooms here (try the Hotel Esperia, tel. 0565 42284, which is picturesquely located on the coast and affords breathtaking night views of Elba); but, on the other hand, there are not a lot of tourists here either. Alternately, you could stay at functional Grosseto, where there are an adequate number of rooms. For those with time to burn, a night or two on Elba could be rewarding. Complete Walk 16 (Parco Naturale della Maremma) during your first day and spend the entire next day on Elba while completing Walk 15 (Monte Capanne to Marciano).

Night 11: Lago Trasemino (Walk 17)

From Piombino to Lago Trasemino, there is no simple, direct route; however, this is your chance to try your navigational skills across Italy's hinterland. Take some time to consult a map and devise a route (figure about 100 miles/3 hours whatever route you decide upon; or by train, transferring to a bus for the 2½ miles uphill to the town center). Castiglione del Lago is an excellent location to pass the night on the lake shore (try the comfortable Hotel Ristorante Trasimeno just south of town, tel. 075 95 21 94) and make ferry connections to unique Isola Maggiore for Walk 17.

Nights 12–14: Assisi (Walks 18–20)

Assisi, one of Italy's most historic and beautiful towns, is well worth the time spent here; however, Gubbio and Spoleto are also attractive towns and, if you have the time, would also merit overnight visits. From Lago Trasemino, take the coastal road to route 75 bis to Perugia, following the signs to Assisi via route 75 (about 60 miles/2 hours; or by train). Numerous hotels catering to pilgrims and tourists are located in and around Assisi; particularly attractive with astonishing views of the surrounding countryside is the Hotel Ristorante Terrazza just beyond the town walls in the direction of Foligno (tel. 075 81 61 42). Take Walk 19 up to Eremo delle Carceri on the first day and complete Walks 18 (Gubbio) and 20 (Spoleto) on the following two days.

Nights 15–17: Rome (Walks 23 and 24)
Rome, the eternal city, can require an eternity for a thorough exploration, and if you have any extra time, Rome is the place to spend it. Rooms abound here, but it is best to avoid lodging in the high-crime area of the main train station, Stazione Termini. If possible, consult a guide book in your price range and reserve ahead. Otherwise the small tourist office opposite track 2 in the Stazione Termini can help you. The strategy of driving around looking for a room, which is acceptable elsewhere in Italy, is quite difficult (but not impossible) in Rome, where the traffic can overwhelm the bewildered tourist. From Assisi (110 miles/3 hours; or by train) take route 75 to Perugia, route 448 to route 204, then A1 to Rome. Explore Rome during the first day and complete Walks 23 and 24 on the subsequent two days.

3. *Rome, the South, and Sicily*

Jump off the plane, hop into your rental car, and skip quickly to the south where great natural beauties, stunning beaches, and monumental historic destinations await. Enjoy long expanses of tourist-free Italy and lower prices while traversing a land of great historic significance. This tour requires more driving than the others, but will introduce you to an enchanting land often ignored on many tours of Italy. Take as much extra time as you can for this tour, stopping as often as possible at both remote and renowned locales along the way.

Night 1: Caserta (Walk 25)

Caserta, close to Rome (about 115 miles/2 hours south via A1) and about 20 miles north of Naples, makes an excellent first stop on your way south. You could stay at Caserta; or, if you prefer, spend two nights at Naples. Tour fascinating Naples on the first day while completing Walk 25 on day 2.

Nights 2–3: Sorrento (Walk 26)

Sorrento is a short hop from Caserta (about 55 miles/2 hours; A1 to A3 to Castellammare di Stabia and then along the coastal road to Sorrento; or by train). If you arrive early, it is possible to visit Capri and Sorrento in a single day; however, Sorrento is an attractive destination and a two-day sojourn here will be quite pleasant. Relax and tour this lovely town on the first day, and visit captivating Capri for Walk 26 on the second day. Hotels abound but tend to be expensive.

Night 4: Amalfi (Walk 27)

The coastal drive from Sorrento to Amalfi (about 35 miles/1½ hours; or by bus) is one of the most scenic in the world and is to be savored. When you arrive, rent one of the numerous rooms in town (try the Hotel Marina Riviera, tel. 089 87 11 04, perched high above the bay, which has well appointed rooms with scenic views), take the bus to Ravello, walk back to Amalfi, and enjoy a quiet evening along the bay.

Night 5: Messina (Walk 28)

You will reach Sicily tonight and, if you have the time, stop at a real, non-touristed Sicilian city. Cruise the *autostrada* and ferry-float to this unique island (coastal road to Salerno then A3 to Villa San Giovanni, where you will catch the ferry to Messina: 290 miles/6 hours; or by bus to Salerno then train/ferry to Messina). Book a room (try the somewhat expensive but convenient Hotel Paradiso in Contemplazione); take a bus that follows the blue waters of the Mediterranean; and walk back along sandy beaches filled with local beach potatoes.

Nights 6–8: Taormina (Walks 29–31)

From Messina, towering Taormina is only a short hop (35 miles via A18; or by train). Book a room (try the elegant Sirius Hotel, which offers astonishing views of the bay and the Mediterranean: tel. 0942 23477). Take the bus to Castelmola on the first day, completing Walk 30. On the second day, enjoy the beaches and Greek ruins at Giardini-Naxos while completing Walk 29. On the final day, drive to Monte Etna and complete Walk 31.

Night 9: Agrigento (Walk 32)

Drive to Agrigento (A18 to Catania, A19 to Caltanissetta, route 640 to Agrigento: 130 miles/3 hours; or by train). Rooms can be hard to find during the summer months, but a quick drive south of Agrigento to Porto Empedocle will probably net you a room in the beach area. Complete Walk 32 during the day and enjoy this lovely town at night.

Nights 10–11: Palermo (Walk 33)

Cruise along back roads from Agrigento to Palermo in the morning (80 miles/3 hours; route 189 to Lercara, route 121 to Palermo; or take the more convoluted route 118 all the way, which passes through famed gangster towns Corleone of *Godfather* infamy and Prizzi of *Prizzi's Honor* notoriety; or by train). Enjoy Palermo on the first day and complete Walk 33 on the second day. If you wish to skip Palermo, try the not-so-elegant-but-the-rooms-have-excellent-views Hotel Belvedere (tel. 0924 33 330) at Castellamare del Golfo, which is close to Walk 33.

Nights 11–12: Polignano sul Mare (Walk 34)

A long drive from Palermo (430 miles/12 hours; A20 to Messina; ferry to Villa San Giovanni, A3 to route 534 to the coastal route 106 to Polignano; or by train) will put you on Italy's stunning Adriatic coast. Travellers who abhor long-distance driving can stop for an evening anywhere along the way, particularly at one of the numerous beach communities. Since you will be arriving late, it may be a good idea to reserve ahead (try the lovely, seaside

Hotel dei Saraceni: tel. 080 741 177). Relax after a long, grim drive on the first night and complete Walk 34 on the second day.

Night 13: Gargano (Walk 35)

Cruise the coast to Vieste (route 16 to just past Barletta to route 159 to route 545 to Manfredonia, and route 89 to Vieste: 120 miles/ 3 hours; although you can reach Vieste via train to Foggia and then by bus, getting to the trail head and back is too difficult if you are using public transportation—this is one walk you may omit if you are using public transportation). Rooms can be difficult to find here during the summer, and you may find yourself stuck with a room that comes with a mandatory dinner. However, this is an alluring peninsula and worth the expense and difficulties for a brief sojourn here. Take Walk 35 during the afternoon and stroll about the waterfront in the evening.

Nights 14–16: Rome (Walks 23 and 24)

Rome, the eternal city, can require an eternity for a thorough exploration, and if you have any extra time, Rome is the place to spend it. Rooms abound here, but it is best to avoid lodging in the high-crime area of the main train station, Stazione Termini. If possible, consult a guide book in your price range and reserve ahead. Otherwise the small tourist office opposite track 2 in the Stazione Termini can help you. The strategy of driving around while looking for a room, which is acceptable elsewhere in Italy, is quite difficult (but not impossible) in Rome, where the traffic can overwhelm the bewildered tourist. From Vieste, complete your tour of the Gargano peninsula and then head for Rome on the *autostrada* (route 89 to A14 north to Pescara to A25 to A24 to Rome). If you have time, consider adding an additional day to your itinerary and completing the challenging Walk 22 at Lido di Casalbordino which you will pass on your way to Rome. Explore Rome during the first day and complete Walks 23 and 24 on the subsequent two days.

Thematic Itineraries

1. Ancient Ruins

Greek and Roman ruins abound in Italy, and you will encounter fantastic remnants of the ancient world on the following walks:

11. Rimini Beach/Town Walk
12. Florence: Fiesole to Ponte a Mensola
18. Monte Ingino to Gubbio
23. Ancient Rome: Caput Mundi
24. Tivoli/Hadrian's Villa
26. Capri: Tiberius's Villa
29. Giardini-Naxos to Taormina
30. Castelmola to Taormina
32. Agrigento: Into the Valley of the Temples

2. Great Castles and Walls

Italy has been invaded by everyone who enjoys brilliant sunlight, great food, and superlative art. The result: castles and walls everywhere. The following walks take you in and around some of the finest fortifications and castles in Italy:

7. Algund to Merano
13. Monte Aperto to Siena
14. Zona di Foci to San Gimignano
17. Lago Trasemino: Isola Maggiore
18. Monte Ingino to Gubbio
19. Eremo delle Carceri to Assisi
20. Monteluco to Spoleto
23. Ancient Rome: Caput Mundi
25. Caserta: The Great Palace
29. Giardini-Naxos to Taormina
30. Castelmola to Taormina

3. Famous Cathedrals, Churches, and Abbeys

Italy has many beautiful and famous cathedrals, churches, and abbeys. The following walks will take you to one of these great monuments:

1. San Fruttuoso to Portofino
6. Oberbozen to Bolzano
12. Florence: Fiesole to Ponte a Mensola
13. Monteaperto to Siena
14. Zona di Foci to San Gimignano
17. Lago Trasemino: Isola Maggiore
18. Monte Ingino to Gubbio
19. Eremo delle Carceri to Assisi
20. Monteluco to Spoleto
23. Ancient Rome: Caput Mundi
34. Abbazia Sán Vito to Polignano sul Mare

4. Fabulous Forests

Although Italy has been largely deforested throughout the ages, many large and verdant woodlands still exist. The following walks will take you into a world of leafy solitude.

1. San Fruttuoso to Portofino
4. Lago Magiore: Cannero to Cannobio
5. Monte Generoso: Vetta to Bellavista
7. Algund to Merano
10. Lago di Garda: Marniga to Castelletto
12. Florence: Fiesole to Ponte a Mensola
15. Island of Elba: Monte Capanne to Marciano
19. Eremo delle Carceri to Assisi
24. Tivoli/Hadrian's Villa
35. Parco Nazionale del Gargano

5. High Hills and Massive Mountains

The following walks capture the scenic splendor of Italy's massive mountains and high hills:

3. Brunate to Como
5. Monte Generoso: Vetta to Bellavista
6. Oberbozen to Bolzano
7. Algund to Merano
8. Dolomites: Ortisei to St. Christina
9. St. Christina to Selva/Wolkenstein
10. Lago di Garda: Marniga to Castelletto
12. Florence: Fiesole to Ponte a Mensola
15. Island of Elba: Monte Capanne to Marciano
18. Monte Ingino to Gubbio
19. Eremo delle Carceri to Assisi
26. Capri: Tiberius's Villa
27. Ravello to Amalfi
30. Castelmola to Taormina
31. Monte Etna

6. Captivating Coasts and Beaches

The following walks take full advantage of Italy's stunningly beautiful coastal scenery:

1. San Fruttuoso to Portofino
2. Cinque Terre: Vernazza to Riomaggiore
11. Rimini: Beach/Town Walk
15. Island of Elba: Monte Capanne to Marciano
16. Parco Naturale della Maremma
21. Mediterranean Pines: Silvi Marina to Pineto
22. Stazione Porto di Vasto to Lido di Casalbordino
26. Capri: Tiberius's Villa
28. Sicily: Straits of Messina
29. Giardini-Naxos to Taormina
33. Riservo di Zingaro
34. Abbazia San Vito to Polignano sul Mare
35. Parco Nazionale del Gargano

7. Inland Waterways

The following walks follow, at least partially, the course of Italy's beautiful lakes, rivers, and canals:

3. Lago Como
4. Lago Maggiore
7. Algund to Merano
10. Lago di Garda
17. Lago Trasemino
25. Caserta: The Great Palace

8. Great Art Centers

Some of the finest art in the world resides in Italy, and the following walks have the added bonus of being near great centers of art:

12. Florence
13. Siena
19. Assisi
23. Ancient Rome: Caput Mundi
33. Riservo di Zingaro (Palermo)

9. The Must-See Itinerary: All the Greatest Sights

If you have a limited time in Italy and wish to see the most famous sites while enjoying a great walk, choose from among the following:

12. Florence: Fiesole to Ponte a Mensola
13. Siena: Monteaperto to Siena
14. Zona di Foci to San Gimignano
19. Eremo delle Carceri to Assisi
23. Ancient Rome: Caput Mundi
24. Tivoli/Hadrian's Villa
26. Capri: Tiberius's Villa
27. Ravello to Amalfi
30. Castelmola to Taormina
32. Agrigento: Into the Valley of the Temples

10. Author's Favorite Walks

The following walks were difficult to select, and they may not include the most famous sights, but in each case the walk itself is superb:

1. Italian Riviera: San Fruttuoso to Portofino
2. Cinque Terre: Vernazza to Riomaggiore
4. Lago Maggiore: Cannero to Cannobio
7. Algund to Merano
10. Lago di Garda: Marniga to Castelletto
15. Island of Elba: Monte Capanne to Marciano
17. Lago Trasemino: Isola Maggiore
19. Eremo delle Carceri to Assisi
23. Ancient Rome: Caput Mundi
27. Ravello to Amalfi

Walks-at-a-Glance

These brief summaries will help you decide which itinerary is best for you or allow you to assemble your own unique itinerary. Full details for each walk can be found in Part Two.

Walk 1 **Italian Riviera:** *San Fruttuoso to Portofino*

Begin this memorable day with a boat ride along a spectacular segment of Mediterranean coast to a medieval monastery that can be reached only by foot or by boat. Stop for a swim and lunch at the diminutive but comely beach; and before venturing into the hills from this rocky cove, take a tour of the Gothic church and its wonderfully preserved cloister. Climb quickly into the forest where views of San Fruttuoso, the Mediterranean Sea, and eventually Portofino are spectacular throughout. Relax, dine, imbibe, and yacht watch along Portofino's pulchritudinous port while rubbing shoulders with millionaire yachtsmen in this carless paradise. If you can, tear yourself away from quiet cafés long enough to visit the sixteenth-century Castello di San Giorgio and perhaps the sixteenth-century parish church of San Martino which houses a few interesting works of art.

Walk 2 Cinque Terre: *Vernazza to Riomaggiore*

Cinque Terre (literally five lands, actually five villages) is a superb collection of five proximate and unique villages lining a rugged section of the Mediterranean coast. Originally these diminutive settlements relied on fishing for their well-being, but recently fishing has become eclipsed by tourism as a raison d'être. However, thanks to the villages' relatively remote location, tourism has not become rampant, and a day strolling through and between these towns will not connect you with the elbows of too many DROPS. Today's walk connects four of these relaxed seaside gems along a centuries-old trail of transhumance that offers for your visual delight continuous, superb coastal views and brilliant effusions of wild flowers. Along the way, enjoy ruined castles, medieval churches, and comely coves while traversing enchanting forests and fertile vineyards. Lunch or beverages are available at lovely seaside cafés in each of the four towns, and, as an added bonus, you may stop for a swim at many points along the way.

Walk 3 Lago Como: *Brunate to Como*

Lake Como is a lovely sight throughout its circumference: towns rise precipitously up steep hills, boats of all descriptions gracefully ply placid waters, and at night the lake shimmers under glistening moonlight while city lights twinkle ad infinitum in the distance. Today's trek begins with a breathtaking funicular ride straight up Como's cliffs to *bella* Brunate which is situated on a hillside terrace where you will enjoy superb views extending as far as Milan on a clear day. Heading downhill, you will savor superb views of the lake and the city of Como while passing a number of magnificent villas which appear to have been built in the late-nineteenth and early-twentieth centuries. As you continue to descend, villas and houses soon disappear, and the trail becomes more rustic in nature. Bustling lakeside Como, the city, is a worthy destination and home to a variety of historic sites that you will want to visit.

Walk 4 **Lago Maggiore:** *Cannero to Cannobio via ferries to and from Luino*

As you ferry across placid waters from Luino to today's trail head, scan the verdant lakeside—you will see not only Cannero but also Cannobio, your starting and stopping points. Between these two lakeside gems, however, there is no indication of the pacific pathway piercing an emerald forest where you will course quickly and alone through an almost forgotten arcadia. Along the way to Cannobio, you will traverse remote farmlands and be stunned by the number of long abandoned stone structures which continue to stand in romantic silence, almost completely obscured by encroaching foliage. You will also enjoy frequent views of the lake and of towns in the distance and be charmed by at least seven waterfalls which tumble white-water rapidly down forested slopes. Having traversed one of the most picturesque trails in Italy, you will arrive at comely Cannobio where you can relax with a beverage along the picturesque waterfront before ferrying back across lovely Lago Maggiore.

Walk 5 Monte Generoso: *A Swiss Excursion: Vetta to Bellavista or Melano*

You will reach the summit (*"vetta"* in Italian) of Monte Generoso, which offers stunning views of both Italy and Switzerland via a spectacular narrow-gauge train excursion. Relax in one of the two restaurants that provide panoramic views and then begin the spectacular descent to Bellavista which provides constantly varying, stupendous views of mountain and valley. If you can unglue your eyes from the horizon, glance along the path itself at the deep stands of wild flowers which brilliantly illuminate your way. The optional remainder of the walk to Melano is an attractive forest trek that takes you through the pretty town of Rovio and along remote trails. The final descent from Rovio again provides excellent views of lake and valley.

Walk 6 Bolzano: *Oberbozen (Soprabolzano) to Bolzano*

Today's admirable amble commences at a tranquil mountain village and descends gloriously to a superb mountain town. After a spectacular cable-car excursion you will arrive at Oberbozen which has all of the accoutrements of a standard Alpine paradise: high-mountain views, quaint Bavarian-style hotels, folksy restaurants catering to hearty *"bier trinkers,"* a narrow-gauge train, cool air on a sunny day, and a sense of quiet serenity. You will descend to elegant, well-appointed, and historic Bolzano amidst panoramas that are ubiquitous and astonishing: city, sky, mountains, rivers all meld into a single tableau of enormous proportions. Try not to be overwhelmed by the immensity of this walk.

Walk 7 Merano: *Algund to Merano*

Inhabited by strong, rosy-cheeked, blond-haired young men and women (Heidi herself would feel at home here), Algund is the typical northern fairy-tale town—cobblestone streets, quaint architecture, and green-mountain ambience; try to restrain yourself from yodelling as you pass through. Ascending from Algund, you will begin a memorable march that will take you through shimmering forests, delightful orchards, and viney vineyards. Approaching Merano, you will traverse the Tappeiner Weg, a world-class promenade enriched by several trail-accessible restaurants, all sporting excellent views of the valley and mountains. The final descent into Merano begins at a well-preserved castle keep (Torre della Polvere) and proceeds along the frigid, fast-flowing waters of the Passirio River directly into elegant Merano's historic Old Town.

Walk 8 Dolomites: *Ortisei to St. Christina*

The Dolomites epitomize the Alpine stereotype of jagged grey peaks standing tall against menacing grey skies; however, on a clear day, golden rays piercing blue skies illuminate the peaks, bathing them in a soft glow that produces a lofty haven of tranquillity. From macho mountain-town Ortisei, you ascend in a rapidly rising cable car that drops you at Seceda, more than eight thousand feet above sea level. From Seceda, you will begin a superbly beautiful walk through alpine meadows surrounded by serrated peaks and green slopes along a trail which is punctuated by flourishes of luminous, multicolored wild flowers. In spite of the high-mountain locale, this is a supremely civilized walk along a trail dotted with restaurants, park benches, and remote huts that can be rented for lonely, on-top-of-the-world experiences.

Walk 9 **A Valley Walk:** *St. Christina to Selva/ Wolkenstein*

St. Christina, embraced by arbor-covered slopes, lies recumbent and tranquil in a cool mountain valley where skiing and hiking reign supreme. Along the way to equally tranquil Selva/Wolkenstein, you will enjoy constantly changing views of the mountains, be treated to the sights and sounds of a copiously flowing white-water river, and be captivated by effusive fields of shimmering wild flowers. There is no finer way to shuttle between towns than this path which alternates between rustic charm and sparsely inhabited resort areas. Combine this walk with Walk 8 for a long but superb day of mountain trekking.

Walk 10 **Lago di Garda:** *Marniga to Castelletto*

Lago di Garda, largest of the Italian lakes, extends gracefully for almost 35 miles amidst an undulating landscape of verdant hills and granite cliffs which drop precipitously into the lake allowing only a thin shore-hugging band of habitation, and a few communities clinging tenuously to the mountains. Today's walk will take you between two lovely little coastal towns, under the shadow of massive Monte Baldo. Ascending steeply from tiny Marniga, you will soon arrive at the mysterious town of Campo, an eerie relic of an almost forgotten past, now hovering in the penumbra of total abandonment. This fascinating jumble of the quick and the dead is one of my favorite trail memories. Continuing along this lovely wild-flowered, forested walk, sheltered by shady trees, and enlivened by the sonorous sounds of omnipresent song birds, you will enjoy excellent views of Lago di Garda and soon arrive at winsome, lakeside Castelletto.

Walk 11 Rimini: *Beach/Town Walk*

What Coney Island used to be to America or what Blackpool is to the English, Rimini is to the Italians. This beach potato's Mecca is truly a unique experience—the epitome of excess in a nation of excess. Trekking along miles of sandy beaches, you will thrill to the world's largest assembly of beach chairs—at least a billion. Shifting to Rimini's main drag: miles of chaos await as you pass a curious melange of low culture, including cut-rate clothing shops, *gelati* joints, pizza parlors, pick-up bars, beach accessory emporiums, leather stores (no restraining devices), sex shops (restraining devices), small amusement parks, tennis courts (for the occasional patrician traveller), disconcerting discotheques, a Roman circus, a winding water slide, and even new- and used-book vendors. This is truly a walk on the wild side.

Walk 12 Florence: *Fiesole to Ponte a Mensola, then to Florence or Settignano*

Before descending to Florence from historic, hill-town Fiesole, you will enjoy stunning multi-directional views into the land of Boccaccio's *Decameron* and lounge leisurely in the rarefied atmosphere. From Fiesole's diminutive town center, you will then pass millenia-old Etruscan tombs and enter a series of narrow roads in a forested world seemingly remote from urban woes but actually only a few miles from bustling Florence. This ethereal forest walk is enhanced by the presence of superb wild flowers, views of distant Tuscan hills, and overpowering panoramas of Florence and its signature Duomo.

Walk 13 Siena: *Monteaperto to Siena*

This pleasant and interesting stroll along a frequently shady, narrow band of asphalt takes you through rolling fields punctuated by a couple of sleepy hamlets. The slow pedestrian pace provides you with an opportunity for a glimpse into the lives of ordinary people who live on the fringes of Sienese culture. Throughout the entire walk, you will be stunned by the views of distant Siena rising majestically from the fertile Tuscan plain, and upon arrival at Siena, you will enter the walls through an impressive medieval gate and enjoy one of Italy's finest cities, which is abundantly endowed with art treasures and architectural masterpieces.

Walk 14 **San Gimignano:** *Zona di Foci to San Gimignano*

Zona di Foci, an area reminiscent of the arid hill country in northern New Mexico, and rural bus stop par excellence, is your in-the-middle-of-nowhere starting point for today's high walk to the lofty towers of San Gimignano. Along the way, you will gaze through vast fields at distant San Gimignano rising regally amidst rolling hills. You will also stroll around villas and through vineyards while enjoying startling effusions of brilliant wild flowers, and dazzling fields of densely packed, domesticated sunflowers. San Gimignano, towered haven for financially elite travellers, is probably the most visually stunning of the Tuscan hill towns, and like many towns in Italy, San Gimignano is itself the main attraction: narrow winding streets, intimate city squares, and tall towers casting long shadows combine to make this small patch of intricate urbanity an enduring visual delight.

Walk 15 **Island of Elba:** *Monte Capanne to Marciano*

Comparable to a sun-drenched Greek island, Elba (where Napoleon was exiled for about a year) is a visual delight: miles of sandy beaches ring a mountainous interior; languid villages slumber lazily though protracted summer days; and constantly changing panoramic vistas astonish at every bend of the road. After a one-hour, panorama-replete bus ride you will be whisked via cable car to the peak of towering Monte Capanne where you can survey the breathtaking spectacle of the entire island. The lovely descent from Elba's highest point is replete with astonishing vistas, beautiful secluded forests, and the preternatural calm of the Elban high country. The final approach into Marciano, through a series of narrow back streets, is truly Europe through the back door.

Walk 16 Parco Naturale della Maremma: *A ramble from Marina di Albarese*

Parco Naturale della Maremma harbors the last unexploited nine miles of Tuscan coast, and it has been claimed that it is also home to the last unspoiled stretch of Mediterranean coast in all of Italy. Departing the rustic beach at Marina di Abarese, you will soon be coursing through a deep-green pine forest where the cicadae sound sonorously and the trees radiate a most fragrant aroma. Emerging from the forest, you will follow the Ombrone River along a sandy bank until you reach the Mediterranean where the sound of cicadae cedes slowly to the crashing of waves driven by fresh winds. From the mouth of the river, you will skirt the Mediterranean coast back to Marina di Albarese. Enjoy a solitary swim and lounge leisurely in the sun far from the madding crowd. This is the utopian way to walk, swim, sunbathe, and picnic the entire day.

Walk 17 Lago Trasimeno: *Isola Maggiore*

Today's adventure unfolds upon Isola Maggiore, largest of Lago Trasimeno's three islands, where you will begin at a painstakingly restored micro-town inhabited by only 60 residents (down from 600 in the sixteenth century) who thrive on a booming tourist industry, supplemented by fishing and crafts. Today's island circumambulation will take you quickly through the town center studded with structures dating back to the twelfth century and past the sixteenth-century church of Buon Gesu, the austere twelfth-century church of San Salvatore, several sandy beaches, a statue of St. Francis of Assisi which commemorates his landing in the year 1211, the fourteenth-century Church of Saint Francis and the Monastery of the Friars Minor Observants. This is a superb excursion, particularly on a sunny afternoon when you may sun, swim, and picnic the day away.

Walk 18 Gubbio: *Monte Ingino to Gubbio*

Gubbio is a lovely red-roofed town that rises in steep terraces beneath the immensity of Monte Ingiño. This relic of a bygone era strongly evokes images of the Middle Ages: stroll picturesque stone streets; inspect medieval ramparts; and visit a variety of historic sites dating back to Roman times. When you are ready for a major out-of-walls experience, hop on the cable car for a quick, spellbinding rise to the top of Monte Ingino where you can visit the impressive Basilica di Sant'Ubaldo. Descending into Gubbio, you will pass through a forest shaded by towering pines, be delighted by a variety of multi-hued wild flowers, and encounter several chapels while savoring soothing silence punctuated only by the occasional sounds of sonorous song birds. The final entry into Gubbio is a joyous experience, as you pass through a medieval gate and encounter almost immediately the impressive cathedral.

Walk 19 **Assisi:** *Eremo delle Carceri to Assisi*

Assisi, a living labyrinth of medieval memorabilia, gently cascades along the slopes of immense Monte Subasio and basks in the glory of some of the finest art anywhere in the world. This pilgrimage destination par excellence will be one of your favorite Italian sojourns; and today's walk, in the footsteps of St. Francis, will take you through a medieval gate, past medieval walls, and along a deeply forested, preternaturally calm trail to the Eremo delle Carceri. The Eremo, frequently visited by Saint Francis for quiet meditation, is a place of surpassing beauty. The lovely, fourteenth-century structures that are open for tourism were not here during Francis's lifetime, but you may visit the cave that contains the saint's rock bed and the small church, cut from rock, that was in existence when Francis visited.

Walk 20 **Spoleto:** *Monteluco to Spoleto*

Spoleto, not far from Assisi and one of the most impressively situated Umbrian hill towns, tumbles gracefully down a heavily forested hill and almost into a deep ravine. This lovely site is covered by a medieval labyrinth of narrow streets, narrower alleyways, and petite plazas where you may repose at a café or wander between impressive monuments of the Middle Ages and Renaissance. When you have exhausted the numerous sites at your disposal but are not yet yourself exhausted, take the bus to Monteluco, a lovely high-country haven of tranquillity, where you may long linger over lovely views of Spoleto and its formidable castle. From Monteluco, you will begin a continuous downhill trek through a deep, quiet forest until you penetrate Spoleto along a medieval daedal of intricately woven passageways.

Walk 21 **Mediterranean Pines:** *Silvi Marina to Pineto*

Silvi Marina and Pineto are basically quiet beach towns without the neon pretensions or frenetic pace of Rimini. This walk will take you along an unusually attractive stretch of the Abruzzi coast and you will follow a beautiful, sandy beach the entire way. Wear your sandals or even go barefoot as you skirt coastal waves; you can stop for swimming and sunning almost anywhere you desire. However, this is not just another pretty beach walk; traversing this very narrow strip of level land between hill and sea, you will have excellent views of the hills and towns in the distance. As an added bonus, one of the finest stretches of coastal pines in Italy parallels the beach.

Walk 22 **A Walk on the Wild Side:** *Stazione Porto di Vasto to Lido di Casalbordino*

Stazione Porto di Vasto is a bleak, modernesque train station serving a vast industrial complex. From here, the initial passage to the sea is not conventionally picturesque, but it is nevertheless an interesting and unusual excursion as you pass through a surrealistic, deep-shadowed industrial zone that harbors factories, warehouses, pollution, etc. Passing quickly without transition from the industrial zone to agricultural fields is unsettling, but you will soon be comforted by the sight of the perfectly pellucid Mediterranean Sea. Coast trekking back to Lido di Casalbordino, you will encounter almost abandoned beaches, negotiate great fields of boulders, scramble over immense numbers of cyclopean concrete pylons, amble through a pine forest along the path of a former rail line, and arrive at a most pleasant beach town.

Walk 23 **Ancient Rome—Caput Mundi:** *A Walk Along the Via Appia Antica into the Center of the Ancient Universe*

Rome, formerly center of the ancient universe and now center of modern Italy, is at or near the top of any short list of not-to-be-missed cities in the world. Today's out-of-walls experience spans one of the world's great archaeological treasures, the Via Appia Antica, where you will trek along a great-stoned ancient thoroughfare and be awed by the remains of tomb after tomb after tomb which line both sides of this remarkable brand of exterior museum. Soon you will reach a series of catacombs which are part of a vast network of subterranean galleries dating back to the third century A.D. that were used for Christian burials and worship. Finally, you will enter Rome, trekking like a Roman past the Baths of Caracalla, the Circus Maximus, the Coliseum, and directly into the great monuments of the Roman Forum. A dazzling assemblage of stellar sights from beginning to end, this is truly one of the most historically significant walks in the world.

Walk 24 **Tivoli/Hadrian's Villa:** *San Polo de Cavalieri to Tivoli*

Imagine yourself not far from Rome at Hadrian's Villa in Tivoli. You will explore the colossal, second-century A.D. Roman palace and then enjoy the lovely, historic town of Tivoli. Unfortunately, as you marvel at a variety of great sights, you will often be shoulder to shoulder with throngs of packaged-tour gawkers.

However, while these hordes of ordinary tourists are shuttled back to Rome, you, the independent walker, will take an obscure local bus to the untouristed, genuinely superlative hilltown of San Polo de Cavalieri. Here, you may have lunch or drink a beverage at a café overlooking an immense, natural tableau before taking the quick, six-mile walk back to Tivoli along a superb cliff-side path with multi-miled, astonishing views of enchanting hills, valleys, and towns.

Walk 25 Caserta: *A Walk from Palazzo Reggia*

Caserta is basically a one-site town, but the single site is superb. Designed to rival Louis XIV's great French folly at Versailles, the royal palace at Caserta is a study in regal ostentation, containing 1200 rooms, 34 staircases, and enough museum-worthy masterpieces of art and furniture to pry open even the most museum-weary eyes. Departing from the palace, you will spy faintly at a distance of two miles a towering waterfall that becomes clearer with your every advancing step. However, you must tear your eyes away from this monumental masterpiece in order to survey the seven superb fountains and twelve little waterfalls that grace your path. At walk's end, you will climb high to the restful sound of water cascading over rock and arrive at a lofty height overlooking the waterfall where distant vistas of the park, palace, and surrounding countryside astonish the worthy viewer.

Walk 26 Capri: *Tiberius's Island of Pleasure: Grotta Azzurra (Blue Grotto) to Capri*

The Isle of Capri has captivated visitors since Roman times, and you may enjoy this tiny, six-mile-long party island in true Roman fashion—baking by day along narrow strands of sand and revelling by night in one of the many discos and clubs that abound around the island. Today's island hop includes all of the major sights, but also takes you way off the beaten Capri path, introducing you to the quiet, seldom seen side of this island paradise. Hydrofoil to Capri; speed-boat to the Blue Grotto; rowboat into the grotto; and then clamber high along a seldom used trail to the lovely town of Anacapri. A steep descent along an almost infinite set of stairs known as the Scala Fenicia and a final approach through a series of back alleys takes you into the city of Capri, an interesting and attractive maze of narrow streets and passageways where you may enjoy fine dining, world-class shopping, and a variety of captivating historical sights.

Walk 27 Amalfi: *Ravello to Amalfi*

The dazzling approach to the town of Amalfi along a road that skirts and at times threatens to drop into the sea is one of the finest panoramic drives in the world. The town of Amalfi was at one time a great maritime trading republic and a rival to Venice and Genoa. Presently, Amalfi's beautiful coastal site, winding, shop-lined passageways, interesting historic sights, and convenient proximity to other, less frequented towns are its main attractions. Today's walk from ravishing Ravello, superbly situated on the heights above the Amalfi coast, will take you along a series of almost-forgotten dirt paths and ancient stone staircases where you may marvel at preternatural panoramas of jagged cliffs, rugged sea, and weatherbeaten villages. The final stage of this distinguished trek involves a passage through maze-like Atrani, a scenic trek along a cliff-side path, and a steep descent along precipitous staircases into the heart of Amalfi.

Walk 28 **Sicily:** *Straits of Messina: Along the beaches north of Messina*

Sicily has hosted such diverse groups as the Greeks, Romans, Carthaginians, Arabs, Normans, French, and Spanish. Remains of these civilizations abound, and this variegated history when combined with Sicily's superb, uncrowded beaches, scenic walks, fine food, and excellent wine produces a traveller's utopia. Today you will enjoy superb views of the toe of the Italian peninsula and the Sicilian hills as you trek along the sandy-beached coast line. You will also enjoy an intimate portrait of the lives of local beach potatoes who bake brazenly under the rays of the meridional sun. Along this rather unkempt littoral, un-svelte and downright fat Sicilians wallow in the sand while ingesting copious amounts of fatty foods. Younger, lankier torsos frolic freely along the surf in anticipation of future fatness. As an added bonus, you can swim at almost any point along this strand, which is way off the beaten tourist track.

Walk 29 **Taormina:** *Giardini-Naxos to Taormina*

Taormina, sublimely situated on a towering promontory overlooking the Ionian Sea, is often considered to be the most beautiful location in all of Sicily. Today's adventure begins with a bus ride to ramshackle Giardini-Naxos, where you may visit a superb archaeological zone that consists of the remains of ancient Naxos, Sicily's oldest Greek colony. After visiting the archaeological site, you will trace the course of the beach, where you may swim at your leisure. If you tire of the beach, the many tacky stores and fast-pasta joints that line the coast road beckon you for a break. Continuing to traverse sand and stone, you will enjoy beautiful views of distant Taormina,

Castelmola perched high above, and other points beyond. Marvel at the multi-miled views; you will soon be back in amply amenitied, historic Taormina.

Walk 30 Taormina: *Castelmola to Taormina*

Today, after a short but tortuous bus ascent, you will visit one of the loveliest hilltop villages in Sicily, Castelmola. Poised precariously on a steep cliff directly above Taormina, Castelmola entices weary travellers with its quiet, medieval passageways which harbor charming shops, commodious cafés, and gracefully aging abodes. There is also a crumbling castle which surveys, from on high, the surrounding countryside. The descent along little-known, convoluted pathways affords admirable views of photogenic Taormina and dazzling vistas of the sea, beaches, towns, etc. in the distance. This is one of the best short walks anywhere.

Walk 31 Monte Etna: *Descent to the Rifugio Sapienza*

Today, you will take a spectacular cable car voyage 8000 feet up the side of jet-black volcano Monte Etna while marvelling at long views of the surrounding lava-layered landscape. From the cable car station, the trail cuts a tortuous swathe through immense piles of lunar-looking rubble. Tons of black lava twisted into a medley of contorted shapes lie casually about the trail. Here and there brilliant patches of wild flowers cling precariously to life, and an amazing number of shiny, happy ladybugs grace this path—watch your step. Your ultimate at-bottom destination is the collection of tacky shops and cheap restaurants known as Rifugio Sapienza. Here you can purchase genuine Etna lava that has been carved into virtually any shape—human, animal, and unidentifiable. You can also relax at a café while imbibing both beverages and superb views.

Walk 32 **Agrigento:** *Into the Valley of the Temples*

Beautifully situated at a commanding height amidst rolling hills of orchards and vineyards, the magnificent ancient Greek ruins of Agrigento are one of Sicily's premier tourist attractions. A quick stroll through the city takes you into the lives of the local inhabitants: women hang laundry across narrow corridors while shouting pleasantries to neighbors; children dash about searching successfully for mischief; and cars careen wildly along passageways almost too narrow for pedestrians. Passing from this urban morass, you will be greeted by overpowering views of the temples, the port of San Leone, and the Mediterranean Sea. Soon you will enter the magnificent temple district where you will stroll through temples along an ancient road that still exhibits the ruts carved by the many ancient carts that used to ply this busy thoroughfare. Glance up to the city of Agrigento and down to the sea; the views are excellent and this ancient encounter, found nowhere else, is superb.

Walk 33 **Riservo di Zingaro (Palermo):** *Along the Mediterranean Coast*

Not far from the concrete and chaos of fascinating Palermo lies the Riservo di Zingaro, a unique haven of solitude dedicated to the preservation of natural beauty and a walker's paradise. From the park office overlooking the deep blue Mediterranean Sea, you will cross a tiny bridge, traverse a rocky tunnel, and slide effortlessly into a quiet automotiveless world seldom encountered in Italy. The rest of the trail hugs the coast and offers uniformly superb, world-class panoramas of crashing waves, craggy coastline, and formidable pinnacles.

Walk 34 **Puglian Coast:** *Abbazia San Vito to Polignano sul Mare*

The Puglian coast lies recumbent for hundreds of miles along the Ionian and Adriatic Seas and forms the heel of the Italian peninsula. The arid, sometimes searing climate invites sunbathing, swimming, and general lethargy; however, when you have had a surfeit of baking and bathing, rouse yourself from somnolent torpidity and trek *con gusto* along a most scenic stretch of meridional seashore. Today's perambulation begins at the medieval abbey of San Vito and traverses a rocky, sometimes crowded beach where you may take advantage of numerous opportunities to swim and mingle with locals at the beach and at a variety of snack shops. In town, you will wander aimlessly about an intricate web of narrow passageways and picturesque *piazze* that comprise Polignano's enchanting medieval quarter. At the cliff-side terminus of this intriguing maze, you will stand rapt in admiration at long views into the deep blue sea.

Walk 35 **Gargano:** *Parco Nazionale del Gargano*

The Gargano promontory, jutting boldly into the Adriatic Sea, forms the spur of the Italian boot and, during the summer, is a beach-lover's utopia. Although increasingly more popular among European tourists, Gargano retains much of its remote charm from the days when it was seldom visited and the main industry was fishing. Today's trek takes you along a remote, seldom-used trail where you will enjoy excellent views of cliffs and sea as you walk high above the Mediterranean. Your destination, the sandy beach at Vignanotica surrounded by steep cliffs and high hills, is quite alluring. However, you will not be alone; a surprising number of beach potatoes arrive by boat on a daily basis, and a snack bar exists for their culinary pleasure. Relax on the beach, enjoy a good swim, and snack heartily before heading back to the trail.

Part One

Hitting the Trail

1. Before You Leave

Other Travel Guides

The stolidly written but very useful green Michelin Guides provide a good general overview of Italy. There is a single book that covers all of Italy and also one that provides a comprehensive description of Rome. Each has a map in the front that rates the importance of all the sites, major and minor, within a certain region. They also have sections relating to history, culture, and specific monuments. I am often surprised to find even the most obscure places mentioned and do not hesitate to consult these guides when I am formulating walking and driving routes. They can be purchased in many American and European bookstores and are moderately priced.

When a travelling companion purchased a *Let's Go: Europe* book in 1985, I humored her by saying that it was a good idea. What I actually thought was that it was a waste of money, and I had nothing to learn from a cabal of callow college students. Before going to Europe that summer I deigned to regard only the book's cover, shunning the contents. Slowly, while driving, as my companion continued to stridently bark out many useful bits of information, I was converted. At first I would steal glances at a page or two; later I found myself reading whole chapters. Now I would consider no trip without a copy. When I read one of these volumes, I want to leap from my couch, strap on a backpack, throw away (or perhaps just hide) my credit cards, and travel cheaply to all of these wonderful and charming places. Of course, the feeling soon passes; I regain my senses; and I check my wallet for the reassuring sight of a credit card. I highly recommend purchasing *Let's Go: Italy* (New York: St. Martin's Press, annual). I have seen no other guide that contains so much information on train/bus schedules, tourist offices, places to change money, laundromats, restaurants, and much more. You would also be wise to purchase the recently cloned *Berkeley Guides: Italy on the Loose* (New York: Fodor's, annual) which successfully emulates the strident stinginess of the *Let's Go* guides while adding valuable information especially for outdoor enthusiasts.

I would also recommend the various guides published by Arthur Frommer, especially if you are looking for more upscale dining and accommodations. However, as I will soon discuss, finding lodging in Italy is usually not a problem.

For fascinating overviews of the history of Italy as it relates to the modern traveller, I strongly recommend Interlink Publishing's *A Traveller's History of Italy*. This compact volume offers a complete and authoritative history from the earliest of times up to the present day. A gazetteer cross-referenced to the main text pinpoints the historical importance of many of the sights and towns you will encounter on your walks.

Until I read Colin Fletcher's *Complete Walker*, my few desultory attempts at backpacking and wilderness walking were singularly unsuccessful. This book changed my walking life and made me a successful outdoorsperson. I hope future editions come bundled with bionic knees which would also help. Even if you are only contemplating a walk through a city park, you will probably find some useful tips. Every conceivable topic is exhaustively treated. I recommend this book for backpackers and day hikers. Wonderfully written in idiosyncratic "old codger" prose, the *Complete Walker III* (New York: Alfred A. Knopf, 1986) should be found in every walker's bookcase.

Language: How Much Is Enough?

Although I read Italian and speak it haltingly, I sometimes have difficulty understanding what people are saying to me. Achieving perfect speech and comprehension is generally unattainable unless you are a specialist in the language and spend much time studying in an immersion environment. Fortunately, fluency in Italian is not an important factor for a successful walking tour of Italy, particularly if you enjoy being lost and unable to communicate with anyone. Actually, since there is usually no one around to interrogate, I can think of no instance where language ability would have meant the difference between being lost or found. Furthermore, if you follow the trail notes contained in this book you should have no problems.

However, since few Italians speak more than a little English, you should attempt to learn the language of your host country. If you are like me and cannot afford a private tutor, the next best technique is to purchase language tapes that are packaged with workbooks. The best material I have found is in Passport Books' Just Listen and Learn series which is available in many bookstores. Many other competently produced series have made an appearance in recent years, and I suggest you peruse the shelves of your local bookstore for a set that will be compatible with your learning style.

Level of Fitness

If you are already a regular walker, you should have no problem with any of the walks listed in this book. None of the walks requires any serious climbing, but a few involve a number of breathtaking ups and downs. In the trail notes, I have listed the approximate amount of climbing that you will do on each trail. If you are not a frequent walker and are not involved in an exercise program, you should begin walking regularly a couple of months before you arrive in Italy. The walks that I have included vary from about two to nine miles, with most ranging from three to six miles. If you can walk four to five miles before you leave, you should be able to complete all of the walks I have listed. There are a number of books that show you how to develop a walking-fitness program. I have never been able to read more than a few pages of such books and find it odd that so much ink has been devoted to such a simple and natural motion. I just begin with a few three-to-five-mile walks and increase the distance until I reach the maximum length of walk that I anticipate completing. At this level of walking fitness, I adjust quickly to walking in Italy.

Car Rental

If you have decided to drive, you should reserve a car before you leave for Italy. Renting a car once you have arrived in Italy is substantially more expensive. I always find the cheapest and most fuel-efficient vehicle. For up to three people who are not large and do not bring much luggage, the smallest vehicles are sufficient. It is best to comparison shop for rates, but I have always found Kemwel to be the least expensive on a long-term basis. The longer you use the car the better the price, and if you lease for a minimum of three weeks you will be able to secure good terms. You can order Kemwel's brochures in the U.S. at 1-800-678-0678. Ask for both the car rental and car lease brochures. When touring Italy, I prefer to arrive at Nice in France, about 30 minutes from the Italian border. Airfares are similar to those for Rome or Milan, but car rental is several hundred dollars less in France.

When to Go

Most people will go during the summer, but Italy's warm climate allows for walking throughout the entire year except in certain mountain regions. On the other hand, be careful to avoid dehydration or sunstroke during Italy's canicular summer months.

What to Bring

Money

With the less-than-impressive dollar hovering around 1600 lire, I budget about $90–100 (£54–60) per day if I am travelling alone (staying in three-star hotels and eating moderately-priced meals). I find that an extra person adds about $40–50 (£25–34) to the expenses, adding up to about $130–150 (£80–95) per day (for information on how to travel more cheaply in this surprisingly expensive land, consult the budget guides mentioned above). I usually carry about $400 (£260) worth of lire in cash for minor purchases or emergencies, and some American Express travellers checks to replenish cash. I charge most meals and hotels since Visa, Mastercard, and American Express cards are accepted almost universally in Italy. However, you should always have some cash in more remote areas and in case computer lines are down and your credit card is not approved.

Luggage

I bring one backpack, which serves as check-in luggage. It carries almost everything except books, guides, maps, and other expensive items. You may wish to purchase a pack that has a disappearing suspension system as an alternative to a wilderness pack. Ordinary luggage with only a handle looks pathetically useless to me and, unless you have porters or are on a guided tour, it should be shunned.

I use what will be my hiking daypack as carry-on luggage. I own a Lowe Klettersack, which is incredibly durable, comfortable, and capacious. My third piece is a small shoulder bag that contains photographic equipment, mini cassette recorder, and a few other small items. When I arrive at the airport or park my car, I put the large pack on my back, strap the camera bag around my neck, hold the daypack with both arms, and stagger to my destination. I avoid bringing more than I can carry in one trip.

Clothing

Including what I am wearing on the plane, I bring four shirts, two pairs of pants, two pairs of shorts, two pairs of regular socks, three pairs of wool hiking socks, four pairs of underpants, one hat, one sweater, one lightweight jacket, one pair of hiking boots, one pair of walking shoes, and one pair of sandals. Everything is color coordinated and can be easily washed and dried. Although I become quickly tired of these clothes, they are sufficient for months of touring and can be easily burned upon return from Italy.

Personal/Health Items

Always bring soap, since some lodgings do not feel obligated to assure that their clients are sparkling clean. I also bring multiple vitamins, which I usually forget to take, razors, scissors, dental floss, thick dental tape which I use to remove trapped, broken dental floss from between my teeth, toothbrush/paste, Ace Bandages for possible sprains, aspirin or aspirin substitute, bandaids, and toilet paper (which is not available at all Italian toilets). I do not bother with shampoo or conditioner, but you may have more hair and find bar-soap to be an inadequate hair cleanser. Female travellers may want to import tampons, which are inordinately expensive in Italy.

Miscellaneous

Sewing needles and thick thread are useful for torn clothes, lost buttons, and damaged equipment. I always bring a high-quality small flashlight that runs on AA batteries to fend off uninvited darkness. An extra, easily-compressed small backpack is convenient for shopping around town and carrying laundry. I also carry a small towel that I have not yet employed for any task; however, I fear excluding it from my pack because I suspect that it will, at an unspecified future date, rescue me from some acute emergency situation. A small am-fm radio may break the silence of a televisionless budget hotel room. A lightweight electronic alarm will prod you from bed and ensure promptness to important transportation occurrences. I never go on any trip, foreign or domestic, without a lightweight goosedown sleeping bag. I have a North Face Light Rider which weighs about two pounds and compresses to almost invisibility. A sleeping bag makes an excellent extra blanket and is indispensable when unrolled in its large storage sack as an extra large pillow which can allow you to sit comfortably upright on a bed with your head against the wall or headboard.

Daypack

On day hikes, I carry a Lowe Klettersac which, as I have mentioned, is strong and durable. It has a top pocket and is also large enough to carry the numerous items I am about to mention. The Klettersac also has a narrow waistbelt which distributes some of the weight from my shoulders to my hips. The waistbelt also prevents the pack from shifting at some critical juncture where I might be sent hurtling into an uninviting abyss. Even if you are not carrying much weight, be certain to purchase a pack with well-padded straps and a waistbelt.

I am not able to enjoy a simple walk without a vast catalogue of items that are designed to ward off any and every conceivable problem. I envy the occasional person I see strolling down a remote trail wearing a disintegrating pair of sandals and carrying nothing more than a leaking bottle of mineral water. I have never had the spiritual levity that allows these people to face possible disaster or even mere discomfort with such nonchalance.

The items you select from the following list for your daypack will depend upon where you fall on the nonchalance/paranoia continuum. I will discuss my rationale for carrying and frequency of use for each item.

The most important item in or on your daypack is water. I prefer the taste of water that is carried in clear, unbreakable lexan bottles with a loop top that prevents the tragedy of lost bottle caps. I use the one-liter size that can be inserted into nylon bottle-holders. The bottle-holders have a velcro loop that can be placed over belts, and I loop one around an adjustment strap on the side of my pack. Depending on the length of the walk, I also carry one or two extra bottles in the pack where they stay cooler. Do not pick up a bottle of mineral water, throw it in your pack, and assume that you have a safe supply of water; they are very flimsy and any dropped pack will mean bottle breakage. Use only indestructible water containers, and do not lose them.

Powdered water additives such as Gatorade can be purchased in many larger supermarkets. They strike me as being expensive, but on longer, electrolyte-unbalancing walks I occasionally use them. They are also useful if you become weary of the taste of plain, warm water.

On most walks, you will carry food. I usually bring some type of whole-grain bread, and I always have a supply of emergency *gauffrettes. Gaufrettes* are the chocolate or vanilla wafers that cause me to gain several pounds during a summer of walking. Most people have more sophisticated culinary desires and will be pleased with the variety of foods available even in smaller stores. For me, picnics involve too much organizing and general psychological stress. However, I realize that not everyone is going to find happiness sitting on a rock while gnawing on a loaf of bread.

I suspect that the concept of ozone depletion is actually a massive conspiracy by the world's sunscreen manufacturers; but, like an atheist who prays occasionally at bedtime, I am not sure and prepare for all possible outcomes. I do not like the slippery feel of sunscreen, and I still cannot bring myself to smear it on my balding, some say bald, head. However, I usually remember to put it on my face and arms. The best I have found is Coppertone's Sport SPF 30 which clings tenaciously to my skin rather than dripping into my eyes. However, if the price escalates from the present $7 (£4) for four ounces, only the wealthiest of walkers will be able to afford its protection. Purchase sunscreen before you leave; in Italy it is even more expensive.

Although I seldom have blisters, I always include a package of Dr. Scholl's moleskin in my daypack. Moleskin and similar products attach to skin in order to prevent sensitive spots from becoming blisters through frequent rubbing against a boot. I have used moleskin on several occasions, and it has saved me from some painful miles. I also carry a small pair of scissors to properly shape the moleskin.

As I mentionedd before, toilet paper should always be kept at arm's reach. There are few toilets on trails and even fewer with toilet paper. Since toilets and reading material are frequently associated items, I should mention that I always bring a book, magazine, or newspaper on a walk. You may be trapped in a situation where you must wait for public transportation, or you may find an alluring spot that begs you to peruse that *Time* magazine whose covers you have been dying to get between.

I have lightweight binoculars that usually stay in my pack. Although they are seldom used, they can be valuable on less-frequently-marked trails that cross many treeless, rockless open fields. Binoculars enable you to scan distant rocks and trees for waymarks.

A mini cassette recorder can be useful for recording thoughts and experiences while on the trail. I also use it to record trail sounds such as singing birds, quick moving rivers, and occasional conversations.

Although it seldom rains in Italy you may wish to pack a poncho or other rain protection; I frequently leave it behind on sunny days. Of course, weather can change quickly in the hills and mountains of Italy and, proving my inability to learn from experience, I have been deeply saturated on several poncholess walks. In cooler weather, I also bring a nylon jacket, which, however, I seldom use.

A map pouch that you can suspend from your body is also indispensable. Silva and other companies make a variety of these pouches which should be waterproof and fasten with velcro tabs. They keep your maps and guides visible but dry and also store a variety of other small items.

Trail Garb: Not GQ

I usually wear lightweight cotton pants and shirts, but during the summer I often wear shorts. Although almost all of the trails in this book are in good condition, your uncovered legs may suffer abrasive attacks on some segments.

Since jogging or walking shoes do not offer tender soles enough protection from the frequently rocky trails, hiking boots usually adorn my valuable feet. I own two pairs of Vasque Sundowners which currently retail for about $170 (£110). They are leather with a waterproof Gore-Tex lining and do not weigh heavily on my feet. They are the most comfortable boots that I have owned, but the soles seem to last only one summer. They can be resoled for about $50 (£35). If you do not currently own hiking boots, I suggest that you try several pairs before making a final decision.

Although I usually wear boots on the trail, I am always in a hurry to remove them when I have completed a walk. If I have a car waiting for me at the end of the trail, I leave a pair of walking shoes or sandals in the trunk and change as soon as possible. If I am taking public transportation back to my hotel, I endure the hiking boots until I return, since they are too bulky to comfortably fit into my daypack.

I have both cotton and wool hiking socks. Both are comfortable, but I almost always wear the wool socks. I have no scientific explanation for this choice. I also have a hat which, unless it is raining, is found in my pack. A poncho and nylon jacket, which I have already mentioned, complete my walking wardrobe.

2. When You Get There

Where to Stay

It is often possible to find a room through the local tourist offices or occasionally via reservations services at airports and train stations. If you feel insecure without prior reservations, check the listings in the guides I have recommended. I do not like to be too precise about when I am going to be somewhere so I generally just look around town when I arrive. Never, even in the height of the summer season at resort areas, have I gone shelterless in this land of abundant accommodations. Usually the first place I check has an available room. However, if you are on a strict budget or are using public transportation to travel around Italy, you may wish to make reservations. I have included some specific recommendations in the Regional Itineraries section that I believe are quite worthy of mention (see pp. 7–17).

Food

The food is fresh, copious, and delicious in this land of epicurean delight; however, if you do not like Italian food, you are out of luck. Ethnic restaurants, especially outside of the major centers, are few and far between. In fact, besides the occasional Chinese restaurant, you will seldom have the option to stray from standard Italian fare. I love Italian food, but after weeks on end it can become monotonous; so as you cruise about, keep your eyes open for something out of the ordinary. However, on the up side, Italian cuisine is vegetarian friendly, and the salads, pastas, gnocchi, risottos, pizzas, etc. are superb, especially when washed down with a hearty local wine.

Public Transportation

Almost all of these linear walks have been designed so that you will have the opportunity to be involved in short trips on public transportation which introduces you into the life of small-town Italy. On rural buses, in particular, you will often believe that you have entered the driver's living room as he is entertaining guests. The regulars converse among themselves and the driver, passing along the latest gossip. Buses, unlike trains, however, are not always on time. Although they almost always appear, you should wait at least 30–40 minutes before abandoning hope. Complete instructions for necessary local transportation are included in the trail notes.

Driving

Even though escape from cars and traffic is one of the goals of a walking vacation, there is no inconsistency in writing about driving in a walking book. Ironically, your car will enable you to more efficiently avoid other cars and also give you the freedom to set your own schedule. You will be free from crowded long-distance public transportation and able to reach places that are not served by public transportation. Although there are some negatives, including expense, heavy traffic, difficult parking in large cities, and the occasional poorly marked road, I would not enjoy Italy as much without the freedom a car allows.

In Italy, you have the wonderful option of enjoying scenic drives through remote villages along lovely secondary roads; however, do not expect to get anywhere expeditiously. Backroads in Italy are sometimes clogged with every sort of lumbering conveyance, from rust-riddled tractors driven by aged, semi-apoplectic octogenarians to hormone crazed pre-teens on mopeds, throttles wide open, noisily attaining dizzying speeds of 30 miles per hour. Endless files of tractors and mopeds represent the worst-case scenario along secondary roads, but you will also enjoy long stretches of quiet country lanes punctuated by lonely villages of ethereal beauty. I prefer these backroads to the harried/hurried lanes of the autostrada where, for a fee, you may drive unimpeded at dangerously high speeds along the length and breadth of Italy. If time is short hurtle down the autostrada; however, if you want to see Italy off the beaten path, cruise slowly along backroads where you will average only about 35–40 miles per hour but be rewarded by indelible images of Italian life.

A final warning about driving in Italy: DRIVE DEFENSIVELY. In Italy, every driver is on a personal mission to circumvent all obstacles in his/her quest to reach a destination. This leads to frequent, aggressive passing and bursts of death defying high speeds. Observing posted speed limits and remaining calm in chaotic traffic are your best defenses. On the autostrada, be content to travel at 75–80 miles per hour, and on other roads simply remember that you are here to see Italy and not engage in Formula 1 racing. However, in many thousands of miles of driving throughout Italy, I have never witnessed a serious accident (although they do occur—watch the Italian evening news for evidence of this). Remember, the cautious driver will escape unscathed the rigors of Italian road wars.

Communication

If you are going to use telephones in Italy, purchase a *carta telephonica* which, unless you are calling an emergency number or the operator, you must insert into almost any pay phone in order to complete a call (although you may occasionally encounter an almost-obsolete, coin-operated model). The least expensive card is 5000 lire. Cards can be purchased at post offices, railroad stations, and many *tabachi* (tobacco stands). Follow the directions on the phone, which will consist of inserting your card and dialing. For long-distance calls to the United States, you may access an American operator from AT&T (172-1011) or MCI (172-1022). Calls cost about $1.25 per minute, so borrow a friend's code number or be prepared to sell personal property when you return from Italy.

Letters take between one to two weeks to reach the U.S. from Italy, if you are lucky. I tried prohibitively priced UPS on one occasion and was astonished to discover that regular Italian mail, at minimal cost, was equally efficient. A sad state of affairs. If you wish to mail a letter or postcard from Italy, go to the local post office or *tabachi* where you may purchase stamps and usually envelopes.

3. Trail Life

Waymarking

Waymarking is the practice of placing indicators (usually a variety of colored paints) on natural objects such as trees or stones to aid hikers in finding their way. Except in the north of Italy, where trails are usually well marked, it is difficult to find suitable trails that are well marked and easy to follow. Most trails, although frequently interesting and beautiful in appearance, are not marked and are often difficult to find even with a topographical map. For example, I searched a variety of possibilities in the arcadian-like Chianti region with every available map for two days only to come up empty-handed. No trail could be easily followed and even local sages, who I assume never bother to walk anyhow, disagreed on where trails went. The situation, however, is improving, and within a decade local walking organizations will have marked many more miles of trails.

The trails in the book represent some of the finest walking available on the European continent, and I have made every effort to find the best trails that are either near great tourist attractions, are attractions themselves—meaning people come to the region to hike—or they take you to interesting off-the-beaten-track areas. The selected trails are either waymarked or easy to follow without being marked. Follow the directions in the trail notes, and you will not get lost. Finally, do not be afraid to get off the beaten path; I have been lost all over Europe and negative events have never occurred. In fact, as you are able to surmise, I have always found my way back. With the aid of this book, you too will always find your way back after many a back-country adventure.

Use of Trail Notes and Optional Maps

All of the walks can be completed without the purchase of additional maps; however, wherever possible, I have recommended maps that will be of use to you, particularly if you are planning to go beyond the walks recommended in this book. All of these maps are topographical, meaning they use what are called "contour lines" to give a detailed picture of how the land is shaped. If you know how to read a topographical map, you will be able to visualize where, how often, and how steeply you must climb on each walk. You will also be able to locate natural features such as lakes and rivers and man-made objects such as buildings and utility wires.

You should also purchase a compass with a transparent, rectangular base plate that can be used in conjunction with a topographical map. They are inexpensive and can always indicate in what direction you are travelling. If you follow the trail notes in this book, you will not need a compass. However, if you experiment with other trails or absent-mindedly wander off the trails described in this book, there is always the possibility of becoming lost. Knowing how to use a map and compass has helped me stay found on a number of occasions. If you purchase a Silva or Sunto brand compass, brief instructions for its use will be included. Study these instructions, and attach them with a rubber band to the compass so that they will be with the compass when you need to review them. There are a number of books that offer instruction in the use of map and compass. *Staying Found* by June Fleming (New York: Vintage, 1982) is clearly written and will teach you more than you ever wished to know about staying found.

If you do not learn from books, try orienteering. This is a rapidly growing international competitive sport. You are given a map and are required to find your way as quickly as possible through varied terrain. Along the way you must record certain codes that will prove that you have touched all points on a required route. There are several levels of competition, and novices are welcome.

For more information, contact the United States Orienteering Federation, P.O. Box 1444, Forest Park, GA 30051.

If you are anxious to order any of the optional maps and guides recommended in the final section prior to arrival in Italy and wish to speak English, telephone the bookstore Edward Stanford Ltd. in London at (171) 836-1321. The staff is quite knowledgeable and they stock a vast selection of maps and guides.

How Often/How Far

I have included walks that are anywhere from two to eight miles, with most in the three-to-six-mile range. Even if you only embark on an occasional short walk, you will experience Italy as have few other foreign tourists.

Do not become obsessed with distance. This is not a competitive sport, and there is no point in consuming entire days with walking. You are on vacation and should enjoy not only the walks but also the destinations. A three-to-six-mile walk will take you into the countryside and onto local public transportation for several hours. You will also get enough exercise to justify a calorie-laden dinner and will be tired enough to sleep well at night. Also remember that you will often be walking several miles around tourist sites and your home base during the evening. A day in which you complete a six-mile walk can easily add up to a ten-mile walking day with such incidental walking.

Time of Day

In less travelled areas, you will occasionally have to arrange your walking schedule around available transportation. However, many areas have excellent public transportation and you can often arrange the walks to fit your general schedule.

When I have a choice, I usually stagger onto the trail at about ten or eleven a.m. This is in contrast to conventional wisdom which counsels early rising in order to beat the midday heat. Since I am never in any hurry to rise early and rush to any destination, I spend many days walking in the noon-day sun with only the occasional mad dog or Englishman as a companion.

Problems

Italy's trails are almost always havens of tranquillity with nothing to fear but fear itself. Although the walker is not yet a familiar sight in Italy, your right to walk unmolested through the countryside is universally respected. You may trek without trepidation.

The Car: Where to Leave It

I prefer to leave the car at my final destination and take the bus or train back to my walk's starting point. This procedure assures me that my car, barring theft, will be there to transport me to my hotel when I have completed a walk. Also, I agonize over problems that might arise with public transportation: a misread or obsolete schedule, a strike, acts of a supreme deity, etc. If you do not cherish the thought of being marooned at walk's end, leave your car at your destination.

Part Two

35 Great Walks

How to Use the 35 Walk Descriptions

Each walk is organized into the following information:

1. **Key to Symbols**: One or more of the following symbols will be found at the beginning of each walk description to give you an idea of what to expect to see along the way:

Abbey/Cathedral

Coast/Beach/Lake

Cable car

Castle

Historic Town Center

Mountains

Villa/Palace

Forest

Art/Museum

2. The **General Description**, which is a short compendium of the topography and historical sites that you will encounter along the route. No attempt has been made to be comprehensive, and it is suggested that you consult the guidebooks mentioned earlier and other sources for more comprehensive historical information.

3. The **Optional Maps** section provides you with maps that may make your walking experience more interesting, especially if you enjoy working with a topographical map or desire to expand your walking adventures in a particular area. Many of these maps and guides can be ordered from Edward Stanford Ltd. as mentioned above (see p. 59). Most of the maps mentioned in this section can be purchased at bookstores in the general area of the walk described. In the north, this is almost always the case; however, as you venture south of Rome, availability becomes less certain. In any case, all of the walks have been designed to preclude the necessity of optional maps.

4. The **Time/Distance** section includes the length of time necessary to complete the walk at a rate of about $2^1/_2$ miles to 3 miles per hour, and the distance in miles and kilometers.

5. The location of **Toilet Facilities** along the trail has been included. Often, however, there are none, which is why information has also been included on the amount of privacy. In general, men should have little trouble relieving themselves anywhere along the trail. On trails where much privacy has been indicated, women should also have no problems. Even where a trail is noted as having little privacy, women will usually have a number of suitable opportunities. Also, remember that you can usually use toilets at bars, restaurants, and train stations.

6. Where you can obtain **Refreshments**, either at a restaurant, café, or bar has also been noted. However, do not neglect to bring water with you on any walk.

7. Instructions on how to arrive at the starting point via automobile and public transportation have been included in the **Getting There** section.

8. The **Trail Notes** correspond to the map, and indicate the general course of the trail. They have been structured so that they may be marked with a check after corresponding landmarks have been achieved. Although the inclusion of a note does not necessarily indicate a problem, notes have been provided wherever problems exist. In any case, always watch for waymarks (when they exist) and study your map.

9. At the end of each section, some **Suggestions for More Walking** have been included. Wherever possible, other day walks have been included, as well as possibilities for shortening or extending each of the 35 selected walks. However, except in the north, organized walking in Italy is still in its infancy and options in many areas may be quite limited.

Walk 1: Italian Riviera

Walk: San Fruttuoso to Portofino

90 mins.
4 miles (6.4 km)

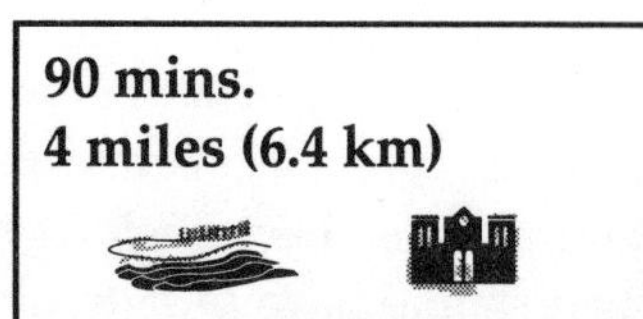

General Description

Begin this memorable day with a boat ride along a spectacular segment of Mediterranean coast to a medieval monastery that can be reached only by foot or by boat—a novel experience in a land where virtually no barrier impedes Italians in clamorous cars from overrunning even the most sacred and lovely areas of this peninsular paradise.

The walk begins at the abbey of San Fruttuoso, where otherwise lonely monks can peer from ornate windows at scantily clad bodies along the slender strand of rocky shore that abuts this venerable religious shrine, producing an incongruent juxtaposition of medieval and modern lifestyles. Stop for a swim and lunch at the diminutive but comely beach; and before venturing into the hills from this rocky cove, take a tour of the Gothic church and its wonderfully preserved cloister.

The climb out of San Fruttuoso is almost 20 minutes of pulse-quickening, shirt-soaking aerobic activity. On the other hand, putting a positive spin on a difficult climb, your ascent is mercifully shaded from the sun, and the views of San Fruttuoso and the Mediterranean Sea are spectacular. The walk along this shady portion of rugged Mediterranean coast (safe from developers' tentacles because it traverses a portion of Parco Regionale Monte de Portofino) is uniformly dazzling and often your only comparisons will be the diminutive lizards that scurry about the trail in multi-colored regalia. Inveterate shoppers will be elated at an unusual opportunity to part ways with their money: about midway along the trail, some enterprising lace-maker/hiker has set up a display where you can purchase some superb locally made designs. Fortunately, I saw no vendors of large appliances anywhere along this otherwise non-commercial trail.

As you approach Portofino, you begin to pass picturesque cottages surrounded by small plots of cultivated earth. The path becomes extremely refined (perhaps pampered yachtsmen use this portion of the trail), with granite stones pleasingly placed for your walking convenience and lined with artfully designed streetlamps for romantic evening strolls. If the stones were yellow, this path would be worthy of Oz. Relax just outside of Portofino in a small church that provides cool shade as a respite from warm sun.

Portofino, protected from automobiles by highly restrictive driving regulations and exorbitant parking fees, has a quiet ambience found in few Italian towns. However, there are few hotels and all are expensive. The cheapest room that I could find was 160,000 lire plus about $20 (£13) per day for parking. Impecunious travellers will want to sojourn at the more plebeian but attractive resort towns of Rappallo or Santa Margherita; both offering lively nightlife and abundant accommodations. As an added bonus, Portofino and San Fruttuoso can be reached by the same boat from both of these towns.

Even if you are not passing the night at Portofino, you should relax, dine, imbibe, and yacht-watch along Portofino's pulchritudinous port and ponder a lost paradise where in times past poor fishermen set out from the tiny cove to earn an honest living. Today, after having sold their in-town property they have all retired as millionaires. Although the Portofino experience is primarily ambience oriented, you will want to tear yourself away from quiet cafés long enough to visit the sixteenth-century Castello di San Giorgio and perhaps the sixteenth-century parish church of San Martino which houses a few interesting works of art.

Optional Maps: Carta dei Sentieri e Rifugi 1:25,000 Appennino Ligure (probably not necessary since the trail is very easy to follow).

Time/Distance: 1 hour 30 minutes/4 miles (6.4 kilometers).

Difficulties: 20-minute climb out of San Fruttuoso, other short ups and downs, and a steep but safe descent into Portofino.

Toilet Facilities: San Fruttuoso, Portofino; some privacy.

Refreshments: Restaurants and cafés at San Fruttuoso and Portofino.

Getting There: Servizio Marittimo del Tigullio boats run hourly (10 a.m. to 4 p.m.: tel. (0185) 77 20 91) from Rapallo, Santa Margherita, or Portofino to San Fruttuoso. Buses also go to Portofino from Santa Margherita (be certain to take the Portofino Mare bus, not Portofino Vetta).

Trail Notes

This trail is marked by two or three solid red circles throughout its entire length. Some signs indicate Portofino Vetta and Portofino Mare; always follow the direction Portofino Mare.

___ 1a. As you exit the boat, follow the signs indicating "Ingresso all' Abbazia," which will take you to the entrance of the abbey.

___ 1b. Exiting the abbey, you will find yourself in a small courtyard where there is a church next to the abbey. There is a

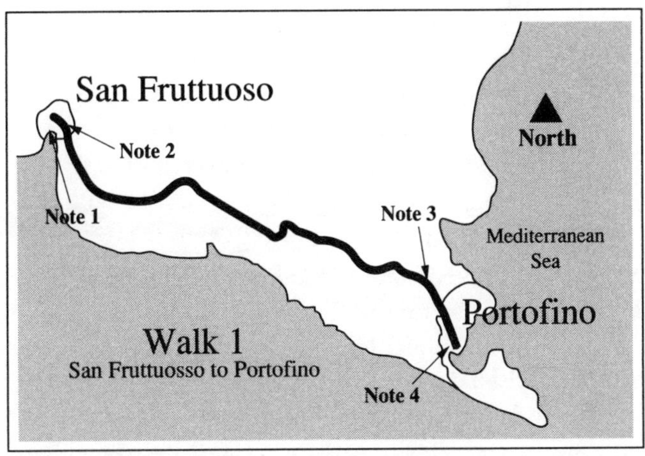

sign "Torre Doria" where you will ascend a stairway and see the first pair of red circles which you will continue to follow.

__ 2. As you pass the first small beach after leaving San Fruttuoso, you will be ascending. Look to your left as you continue upward for the two red circles. This turn is clearly marked but easy to miss if you are in a state of rapt astonishment gazing at the distractingly beautiful scenery.

__ 3. When you see a sign "Portofino Mare 10 min.," bear to the right of the fork that is directly ahead.

__ 4. When you enter the town you will see a set of signs: one indicates "Teatrino." Follow this arrow down to the port.

Suggestions for More Walking

Using the above-mentioned map, it is possible to walk from San Fruttuoso to Santa Margherita or from Portofino to Santa Margherita. Both are slightly longer and more difficult to follow than the walk discussed above but equally scenic. If you are staying in Rapallo, try taking the cable car up to Montallegro and walking down seldom-used country roads while enjoying stupendous views of the Mediterranean Sea and Rapallo.

Walk 2: Cinque Terre

Walk: Vernazza to Riomaggiore

120 mins.
6.2 miles (10 km)

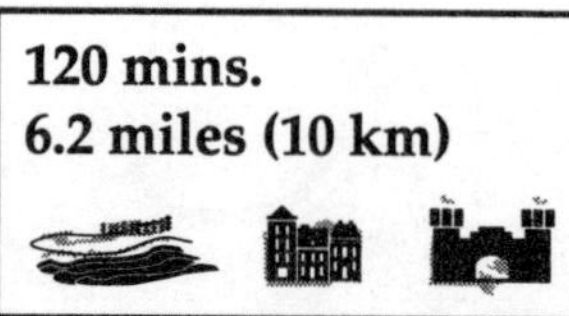

General Description

Cinque Terre (literally five lands, actually five villages) is a superb collection of five proximate and unique villages lining a rugged section of the Mediterranean coast. Originally these diminutive settlements relied on fishing for their well-being, but recently fishing has become eclipsed by tourism as a raison d'être. However, thanks to the villages' relatively remote location, tourism has not become rampant, and a day strolling through and between these towns will not connect you with the elbows of too many DROPS. All of the villages are connected by a tortuous, not-easily-negotiated sliver of a road; if you wish to avoid a generally slow but difficult drive (punctuated by occasional moments of whiteknuckle terror) connect these dot-like towns with your feet or take the local train.

Today's walk connects four of these relaxed seaside gems (vehicles are not allowed in the main areas of these towns, assuring both tranquillity and breathable air) along a centuries-old trail of transhumance. All of the towns rise precipitously from the azure-blue waters of the Mediterranean Sea and are worthy of a brief tour or lunch.

The trail, well groomed and easy to follow throughout, offers for your visual delight continuous, superb coastal views and brilliant effusions of wild flowers. From time to time you will see small motorboats plying their way from town to town carrying passengers; hopefully the singing boatman will pass your way crooning to the rocks in stentorian tones. Occasionally, tear your eyes from the sea and glance over your shoulder to the lovely terrace farms, consisting mostly of vines, that rise gracefully from coastal rocks covering every cultivable square inch of this precipitous land. You may stop for a swim at many points along the

way, but the beaches throughout are quite rocky and many crowded sunbathers are strewn about on rocks in the most improbable places.

The walk begins at Vernazza where there is a lovely harbor and a small beach. A ruined castle looms over the harbor, jutting impressively into the sea, and a picturesque medieval church continues to stand in pious defiance of the march of time. As you ascend from the village via an ancient stone staircase, you will be rewarded by astonishing views of Vernazza and the Mediterranean Sea; soon, in the distance, Corniglia comes into view. However, before you arrive at Corniglia, you will enter a beautiful, enchanted forest permeated with the ethereal sounds of lovely songbirds. The forest quickly cedes to ubiquitous vineyards as you pass along a narrow path surrounded by ancient stone walls on both sides. Comely Corniglia is a quiet, carless town endowed with cool narrow corridors, brilliant flowers, and gardens everywhere. Diminutive plazas lined with small, welcoming restaurants and cafés entice the weary walker. Passing from Corniglia in the direction of the train station, you will shuffle down more stairs than are found on the side of a Mayan pyramid. Cliff-hanging Manarola quickly appears as you continue along this trail of spectacular vistas. Perhaps more frequented than Corniglia but still not overly congested, Manarola's structures tumble chaotically into the picturesque port where you may enjoy a beverage at one of the inviting cafés.

The final, short segment of the trail continues to skirt the coast from Manarola along the via dell'Amore (path of love), which in part traverses an attractive, long concrete gallery that displays murals of lovers in a variety of poses and styles painted by local artists. This most travelled portion of the trail terminates at Riomaggiore, where you can tour the town and take the train back to your starting point.

Do not forget to bring a camera and plenty of film on this walk: point and shoot anywhere for a priceless masterpiece.

Optional Maps: Carte Turistiche e dei Sentieri 1:50,000 Cinque Terre (F.M.B. is the publisher).

Time/Distance: 2 hours/6.2 miles (10 kilometers).

Difficulties: Two eight-minute climbs ascending from Vernazza, and occasional ups and downs throughout.

Toilet Facilities: At railway stations in all towns and many cafés throughout; some privacy.

Refreshments: Cafés, stores, and restaurants in all four towns.

Getting There: All of the towns of Cinque Terre are on the rail line from Genoa to La Spezia. You could stay anywhere along this line and complete these walks and return to base in a reasonable amount of time. Given the difficult nature of driving in this area, use of a car is not counselled unless you stay in one of the Cinque Terre towns. Rapallo or Santa Margherita (mentioned in Walk 1) make a good base for completing both Walks 1 and 2.

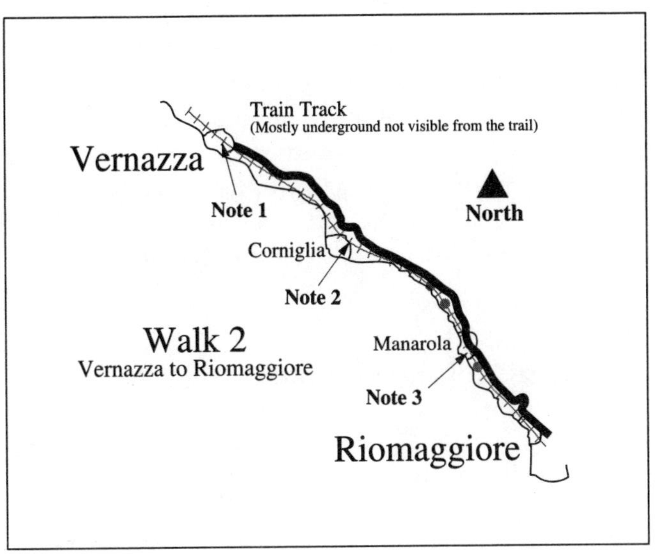

Trail Notes

This trail is waymarked with blue and white bars.

__ 1a. From the train station at Vernazza walk down the main road (the only commercial road) in the direction of the port.

__ 1b. As you walk down this road, look to your left and you will see a stairway with a sign affixed indicating "Corniglia." You will also see a white and blue waymark. Turn left here and begin your ascent out of Vernazza.

__ 2a. After visiting Corniglia, follow the signs to the train station.

__ 2b. The trail continues behind the train station.

__ 3. When you arrive at Manarola, turn left down the main street which is lined with restaurants and stores and follow it as it crosses over the train tracks where you will follow the signs for Via dell'Amore.

Suggestions for More Walking

To shorten this walk you may do any of the following segments: Vernazza to Corniglia: one hour; Corniglia to Manarola: 40 minutes; Manarola to Riomaggiore: 20 minutes. The train stops at all of these towns. If you wish to lengthen the walk, start at Levanto or Monte Rosso, north of Vernazza. In fact, there are many trails (marked and unmarked) in this area and the above-mentioned map provides routes and descriptions (only in Italian).

Walk 3: Lago Como

Walk: Brunate to Como

50 mins.
2.2 miles (3.5 km)

General Description

Lake Como is a lovely sight throughout its circumference: towns rise precipitously up steep hills, boats of all descriptions gracefully ply placid waters, and at night the lake shimmers under glistening moonlight while city lights twinkle ad infinitum in the distance. Wherever you elect to stay along its shores you will be impressed and delighted.

Como (the town), only 40 minutes from Milan by train or quickly reached by the *autostrada,* is a worthy destination in itself or a good side trip for urban-weary Milano visitors. Attractively situated at the southern tip of Lake Como, Como (which is the name of both the lake and the city on its southern shore which was formerly the Roman city Comum and home to both Pliny the Elder and Younger) is surrounded by impressively rocky heights which form a scenic backdrop for this popular resort town. There are several worthy sites at Como, including the all-marble cathedral, which was built over several hundred years beginning in the late fourteenth century, Castel Baradello, built by Frederick Barbarossa in the twelfth century, and the Romanesque style Sant'Abbondio. High-voltage lovers will delight in the Tempio Voltiano and its adjoining museum, which houses a variety of electrifying exhibits in honor of Como native Alessandro Volta.

Today's trek begins with a breathtaking funicular ride straight up Como's cliffs to *bella* Brunate which is situated on a hillside terrace where you will enjoy superb views extending as far as Milan on a clear day. You may wish to linger at this minute patch of urbanity for a few minutes, exploring the few shops, having a drink, or absorbing the views. Leaving Brunate, you will pass a series of magnificent villas which appear to have been built in the late-nineteenth and early-twentieth centuries. The Villa Pirotta is especially opulent. Between villas, there are superb views of the town, the lake, and the mountains in the background. As you continue to descend, villas and houses soon disappear, and the trail becomes more rustic in nature. You will enjoy bucolic serenity and excellent vistas along this serpentine refuge from Italian urbanity all the way into bustling Como.

Optional Maps: Any city map of Como.

Time/Distance: 50 minutes/2.2 miles (3.5 kilometers).

Difficulties: The constant descent will give your legs a good workout.

Toilet Facilities: None, except at cafés in Brunate and Como; some privacy.

Refreshments: Cafés, restaurants, and stores at Brunate and Como.

Getting There: The funicular is located at Piazza de Gaspari, just north of the bus station. Watch for the brown funicular signs that will guide you there. If you park here, you must pay; there is an ever-vigilant attendant.

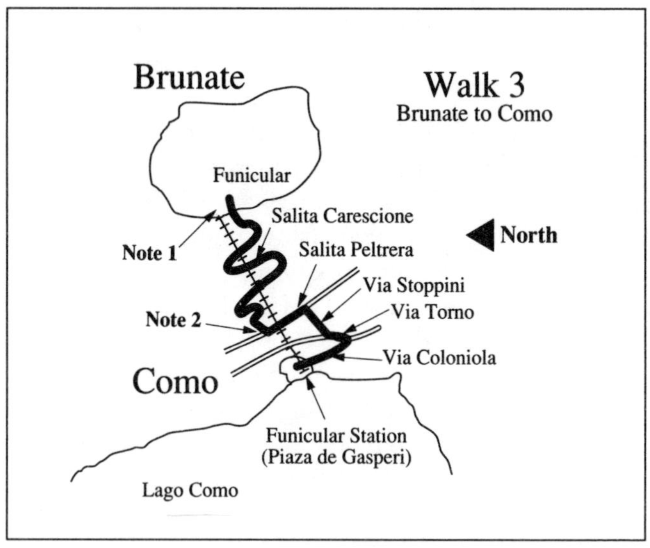

Trail Notes

This is a good time to tour the city as you complete the descent from Brunate. Bring a city map and enjoy this lovely town. There are no waymarks.

__ 1. As you leave the funicular station, cross the road and turn left. Almost instantly, you will turn right at a store where you will see a yellow sign indicating "Pedonale per Como." Just continue to follow this narrow road as it continues downhill; you will see an occasional "Pedonale per Como" sign.

__ 2a. When you dead end at a city street, you will notice a street sign indicating "Salita Carescione," which is the road that you have been walking along.

__ 2b. Turn left on Salita Peltrera, which is the street where you have dead ended (there is no sign here indicating the street name), and then turn right on the first street, "via Stoppini." Take the first left onto via Torno, and then the first right onto via Coloniola which takes you back to the funicular.

Suggestions for More Walking

Masochists or those who enter stair climbing contests will want to walk up the hill and take the funicular down. If you are staying in Como for a while, take the funicular up to Brunate again, where there are a variety of trails. Pick up the Kompass Map #91: Lago di Como/Lago di Lugano at the little store next to the funicular station, and choose a circular route. The trails marked in red dashes do not seem to really exist. Stick to the trails indicated by solid red lines.

Walk 4: Lago Maggiore

Walk: Cannero to Cannobio via ferries to and from Luino

120 mins.
5.5 miles (9 km)

General Description

Lago Maggiore, second largest of the northern Italian lakes, slinks slimly for 41 miles across the Italian frontier and into Switzerland. The leafy banks of this regal relic of the Ice Age conceal one of the finest trails in Italy. As you ferry across placid waters from Luino to today's trail head, scan the verdant lakeside—you will see not only Cannero but also Cannobio, your starting and stopping points. Between these two lakeside gems, however, there is no indication of the pacific pathway piercing an emerald forest where you will course quickly and alone through an almost forgotten arcadia.

Just before arrival in Cannero, the hydrofoil will pass two fifteenth-century fortified island castles which at one time were linked by a drawbridge and used as a base for local pirates. The piracy was finally terminated by the Duke of Milan after a two-year siege of these tiny islands which are currently held in private ownership and not open for public visitation.

Nestled in comely disarray around a quiet harbor and along the banks of Lago Maggiore, Cannero is a tranquil haven where several blissful nights could be passed in one of the several hotels. There are also restaurants and a few shops to help you while away the hours. Departing Cannero, you will scurry along narrow streets lined with ancient but sturdy grey stone structures that are occasionally punctuated by small patches of brilliant floral effusion.

A stone staircase ascending into a dense forest will lead you away from civilization and onto ancient tracks that once formed the network of trade routes in this isolated region. Along the way to Cannobio, you will traverse remote farmlands and be stunned by the number of long abandoned stone structures which continue to stand in romantic silence, almost completely obscured by encroaching foliage. Who were the erstwhile inhabitants? What lives did they enjoy or perhaps only endure? Why were these once lively abodes abandoned? Why am I thinking these thoughts? Such questions will rise frequently to consciousness.

Continuing along this boulder-strewn path, you will enjoy frequent views of the lake and also of towns in the distance. You will also be charmed by at least seven waterfalls which tumble white-water rapidly down forested slopes. Carmine Superiore, about midway, radiates ethereal beauty as it stands firm against the march of time. You will pause breathless in wonder as you pass through the town's deep shadows cast by ancient buildings—the church is from the fourteenth century and many of the homes, though not nearly as old, appear to have been around to witness the church's construction.

Not far beyond Carmine Superiore, the track begins to slowly descend into Cannobio; excellent vistas continue to abound. You will soon enter Cannobio and amble through a most pleasant old quarter and finally to the harbor where you will take the hydrofoil back to Luino. Before departing, pause at the local church, Santuario della Pieta, where, according to tradition, in 1522 a painting of the Pietà shed tears of the blood from the wounds of

Jesus. The painting can still be seen but it has not bled in several centuries. You may also purchase souvenirs along the shop-lined main street or relax with a beverage along the picturesque waterfront.

Optional Maps: Kompass Map #91: Lago Maggiore/Lago di Varese.

Time/Distance: 2 hours/5.5 miles (9 kilometers).

Difficulties: About 10 minutes total climbing from Cannero and another 20 minutes from Carmine Superiore.

Toilet Facilities: Only at cafés in Cannero and Cannobio; some privacy.

Refreshments: Cafés, stores, and restaurants at both towns.

Getting There: The starting point is Luino on the eastern shore of Lago Maggiore. From here, ferries transport people to and from both Cannero and Cannobio. Take one of the frequent ferries to Cannero. Alternately, a regular bus service connects Cannero and Cannobio. If you prefer, leave your car at Cannobio; take the bus to Cannero; and walk back to your car.

Trail Notes

Red and white waymarks mark the path throughout its length.

___ 1a. From the harbor at Cannero, turn left and then take a quick right on the first street going up, via Guglielmo Marconi.

___ 1b. Continue along via Guglielmo Marconi a short distance until you reach a small store called Mini Market; you will see a little sign "via Magg. Gildo Carones," where you will turn right. Turn right again at via Lauro Motegezza which you follow back down to the shore where you turn left and walk out of town. (Trouble following complicated directions? Just walk straight up to the main inter-city road; turn right; and follow the rest of the directions.)

___ 2. When you arrive at the main road, look to your left; you

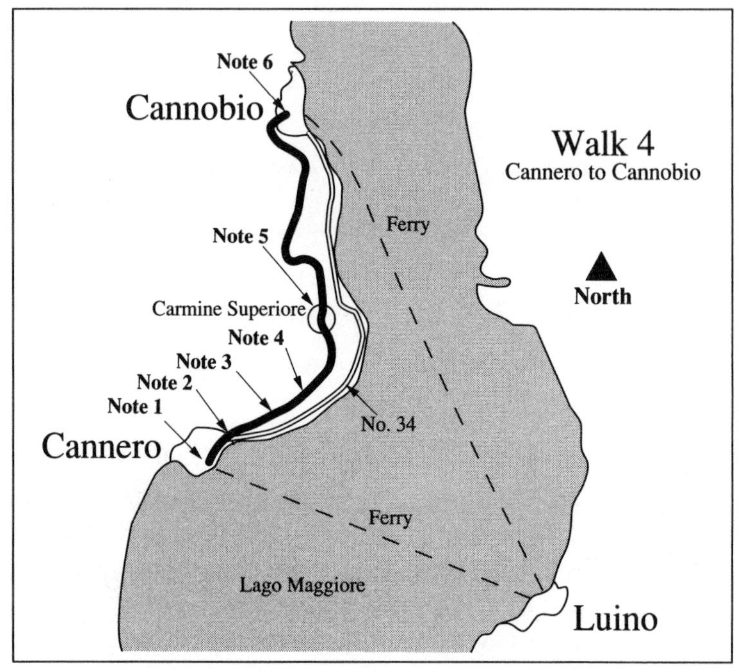

will see a sign "Cannobio 2 h. 10 min." and also the red and white waymarks leading you up a long, stone staircase.

___ 3. When you come to the first fork, just past a sign that indicates "Carmine Sup.," go to your right.

___ 4. At the second fork, be sure to go left to Carmine Superiore. A signpost is visible.

___ 5a. When you reach Carmine Superiore, follow the sign for "Carmine Inf." and waymarks through the town.

___ 5b. At the other end of the town, you will come to a fork; go to your left where you see a park bench and a sign indicating both "Mulinese" and "Cannobio."

___ 6a. When you reach the first vehicular road, turn right and walk into town, making your way towards the church.

__ 6b. To reach the port simply turn right again on the only major commercial street just before the church, via Umberto.

Suggestions for More Walking

Although there is no possibility of lengthening or shortening this trail, there are numerous trails in the area above both towns. Purchase the map mentioned above in order to examine your options.

Walk 5: Monte Generoso: A Swiss Excursion

Walk: Vetta to Bellavista or Melano

45 or 165 mins.
1.8 or 6 miles (3 or 10 km)

General Description

The summit (*"vetta"* in Italian) of Monte Generoso offers stunning views of both Italy and Switzerland. You could reach this venerable apex after a several-hour, leg-warping uphill trek or enjoy the saner (but more expensive) train ride. I elected to train to the top and did not regret lost hours of difficult climbing. I also enjoyed sitting in the train during the steep climb from the train station which imparts the impression of flying rather than passing along narrow-gauge bands of metal up a mountain. The views here are breathtaking as you pass perilously close to precipitous cliffs.

Before descending from Vetta, the summit, relax in one of the two restaurants that provide panoramic views. Only when you have had ample time to absorb distant splendor should you begin the spectacular descent to Bellavista which provides constantly varying, stupendous views of mountain and valley. If you can unglue your eyes from the horizon, glance along the path itself at the deep stands of wild flowers which brilliantly illuminate your way.

Although the best views are on the path from Vetta to Bellavista, the optional remainder of the walk to Melano is an attractive forest trek that takes you through the pretty town of Rovio and along remote trails. As a special bonus, you will encounter a mountain refuge about halfway to Rovio where you can buy refreshments and enjoy a beautiful Alpine meadow. From the mountain refuge, there are occasional lake views as you continue along the tranquil trail. You will soon arrive at Rovio, which is nestled peacefully in a green valley overlooking Lago Maggiore and offers drinking and dining opportunities. Enjoy the final descent from Rovio which again provides excellent views of lake and valley.

Remember you will be in Switzerland. You can pay for the train with a major credit card, but will be unable to make small purchases unless you bring some Swiss francs with you. Change some money at the border when you arrive and be forewarned, like everything in Switzerland, the train ride is spectacular but expensive (about $40 [£23] round trip or about $30 [£17] one way) which is one reason you are provided with a long way down to save money and also to get your money's worth with a longer walk.

Optional Maps: Kompass Carta Turistica #91 (1:50,000) Lago di Como/Lago di Lugano, or you can purchase the map "Itinerari Consigliati" (1:25,000) at the station (3 Swiss francs).

Time/Distance: Bellavista 45 minutes/1.8 miles (3 kilometers); Melano 2 hours 45 minutes/6 miles (10 kilometers).

Difficulties: None to Bellavista; sometimes steep and/or slippery descent to Melano.

Toilet Facilities: Vetta; not much privacy to Bellavista but substantial privacy afterwards.

Refreshments: Vetta, Bellavista.

Getting There: Capolago is at the southern tip of Lago Maggiore and is not far from Como, where you can take a bus. The train

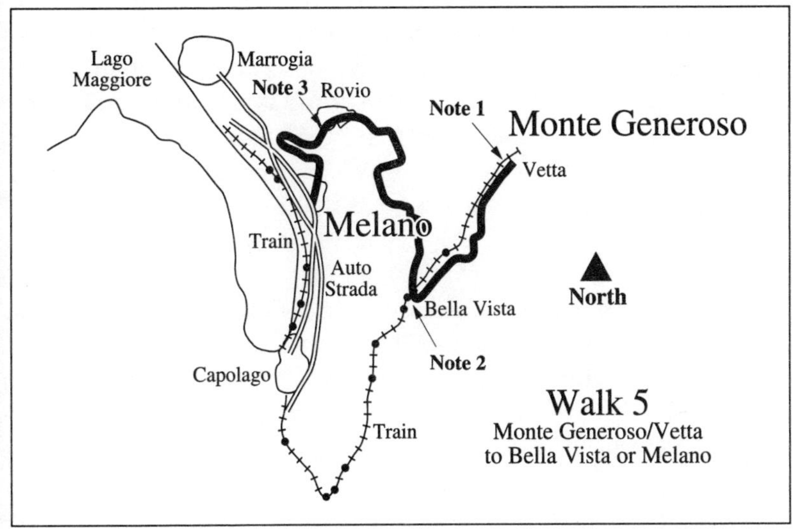

departs from the Capolago train station every 30 to 60 minutes in the morning starting at 9:45 and every 60 to 90 minutes in the afternoon. For information, telephone Ferrovia Monte Generoso at (004191) 48 11 05. If you are taking the optional walk to Melano, leave your car at Melano (the bus stop is just behind the main road and buses pass by every 60 to 90 minutes) and take a bus to Capolago. If you do not have a car, you will have to walk another 35 minutes back to Capolago.

Trail Notes

__ 1. When you exit the train, follow the signposts indicating "Bellavista Stazione." If you plan to take the train back down from Bellavista, you will have no trouble finding your way. Read no further.

If you are going on to Melano read the following (remember the trail can be steep and/or slippery: watch for roots, leaves, stones, etc.):

__ 2. Just before you arrive at the station at Bellavista you will see a sign that indicates "Rovio." Follow the indicated path which is waymarked with red and white bars.

__ 3. When you reach Rovio, just keep descending until you reach the small town center where there is a church and some commerce. You will see a sign on the church indicating "Maroggio 35 min." where you will continue downhill on the asphalt vehicular road until you reach Melano.

Suggestions for More Walking

Both of the optional maps listed above indicate paths for numerous trails from Monte Generoso. There are a couple of longer walks that end in Mendrisio (where there is a train station) that look promising.

Walk 6: Bolzano

Walk: Oberbozen (Soprabolzano) to Bolzano

100 mins.
5 miles (8 km)

General Description

Today's admirable amble commences at a tranquil mountain village and descends gloriously to a superb mountain town. After a spectacular cable car excursion you will arrive at Oberbozen, also known as Soprabolzano (the former name is German and the latter Italian—both "ober" and "sopra" mean above—ensuring that no one's feelings get hurt in this bilingual community). Oberbozen (as it is usually called) has all of the accoutrements of a standard Alpine paradise: high-mountain views, quaint Bavarian-style hotels, folksy restaurants catering to hearty *"bier trinkers,"* a narrow-gauge train, cool air on a sunny day, and a sense of quiet serenity. The only missing factor is Julie Andrews crooning "The hills are alive with the sound of music" as you prance merrily along mountaintops. If you are staying a while in the area and want to be out of the mainstream, this is definitely the place to be.

You begin your descent in rustic reminiscence of bygone times: farmers gather hay, ponies wander about, and fertile fields await fall's gathering. As you continue to descend, watch along the side of the trail for the enshrined photograph of Adempiendo Dovere who lost his life here at the age of 38 in 1965. Circumstances are not embellished; perhaps it was a farm accident. (You will see many such shrines throughout Italy constructed along roadsides where people were killed in traffic accidents—a solemn reminder to be careful anywhere cars go in Italy.) However, what is most impressive is that fresh flowers adorned the shrine as I passed; someone stills loves Adempiendo. Farther along, you will walk through a shady forest for about 35 minutes with occasional distant views as the forest thins. After emerging from the forest, most of the walk is studded with sensational views, and as you approach Bolzano stunning panoramas are ubiquitous and astonishing: city, sky, mountains, rivers all meld into a single tableau of enormous proportions. Just outside of Bolzano you will pass along florid lanes through Eberle, a lovely little village remarkable for its high-steepled church which you have been admiring on the way down.

Bolzano, your destination, is an elegant Swiss-style city that only grudgingly acknowledges its Italian citizenship by allowing a few (very few) token pizzerias. German is spoken first almost everywhere, but almost everyone can also speak Italian. Very elegant in appearance, quite calm, but also situated at the intersection of several major roads, Bolzano makes an excellent base for regional exploration.

Most of the sights center around the Piazza Walther and the elegant avenues to the north. Visit the impressive Gothic cathedral which was constructed between the thirteenth and fifteenth centuries and then head north to the via dei Portici which is lined with expensive shops catering to well-heeled German tourists—if you are in the market for upscale souvenirs, this is the place to shop. The Municipal Museum, which houses interesting peasant-house interiors and traditional costumes, is also worth a quick stop. A couple of castles, Castel Mareccio and Castel Roncolo, will not take you too far out of your way and merit at least a casual inspection. There is a lot to see and do in Bolzano, and the tourist office will be certain that you are well informed; however, it is the views and the hiking that are the most rewarding. You will not be disappointed.

Optional Maps: Kompass #56 Sarntal Val Sarentino (1:35,000).

Time/Distance: 1 hour 40 minutes/5 miles (8 kilometers).

Difficulties: A long downhill walk which can result in frontal thigh fatigue; you will be glad to hit level ground. (Consider the alternative: going up the hill to Oberbozen; I shudder and lose my breath at the very thought.)

Toilet Facilities: Bolzano, Oberbozen.

Refreshments: Cafés and restaurants in both towns.

Getting There: The funicular station is about 1/4 mile east of the train station.

Trail Notes

__ 1a. From the funicular station walk up to the brick street and turn left (do not take the path that descends parallel to the funicular).

__ 1b. Continue on that road for a couple of minutes until you see a red and white sign with a number 6 indicating "Bozen 2 hours," where you will turn left. Continue to follow the red and white waymarks into Bolzano (watch carefully at all junctures when you are in the forested part of the walk; the trail is well marked, but it is possible to walk by some of the turns).

__ 2. When you reach a main street, turn right and follow this street as it curves left to the funicular station. You can see the funicular cables above, which will give you guidance.

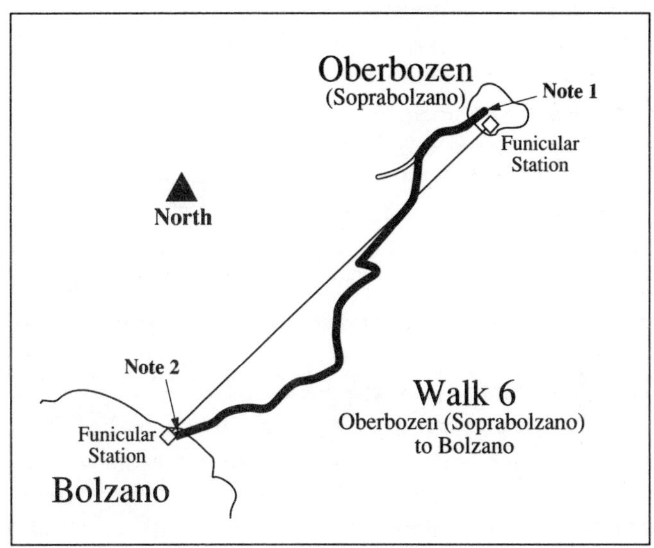

Suggestions for More Walking

There are numerous walks in the vicinity of Bolzano. The optional map mentioned above or any other topographical map of the area will indicate specific trails. Also, there is a multi-lingual Alpinist stationed in the tourist office who can make excellent recommendations for walks of any level of difficulty. In particular, you may wish to take the funicular back up to the train station at Oberbozen and then take the train to Klobenstein from where you can walk back to Oberbozen along various routes.

Walk 7: Merano

100 mins.
5 miles (8 km)

Walk: Algund to Merano

General Description

Inhabited by strong, rosy-cheeked, blond-haired young men and women (Heidi herself would feel at home here), Algund is the typical northern fairy-tale town—cobblestone streets, quaint architecture, and green-mountain ambience; try to restrain yourself from yodelling as you pass through. After strolling about this valley paradise, you will ascend along a shady, vine-covered path which, when bathed in warm solar rays, shimmers emerald green and produces a dappled, Impressionistic visual delight. Soon, numerous fruit trees and ubiquitous grape vines along the now level path combine with distant views of mountain and valley to produce a stunning and venerable tableau of this Alpine arcadia.

The initial portion of the walk takes place along the Algunder Waalweg. (*Waales* are irrigation systems that capture melting snow and channel it to orchards and vineyards along terraced hills and in valleys. Trails that run parallel to a *waale* are called *waalwegs*.) About midway on this *waalweg* you will be greeted by a magnificent castle (Schloss Thurnstein) set high on a rocky roost above a terraced treasure of a town that slinks gracefully down a gentle wooded slope.

Departing the Algunder Waalweg, you will soon enter the enchanting and famous Tappeiner Weg (named after Dr. Tappeiner who generously donated this land to the city after his death around the turn of the century), which will take you along a superb route directly into most elegant Merano. Botanists will be impressed by the detailed map (which indicates the position of dozens of forms of plant life and labels them in Latin) which marks the entrance to the Tappeiner Weg. People of all ages and body types ply their way slowly along this shady band of rural tranquility. Park benches are strategically placed in scenic locations where strollers enjoy superb views while ingesting voluminous picnic lunches. This is truly a world-class walk enriched by several trail-accessible restaurants, all sporting excellent views of the valley and mountains. Linger at one of the restaurants or repose thriftily on a bench, but hasten not from this serene setting.

The final descent into Merano begins at a well-preserved castle keep (Torre della Polvere) and proceeds along the frigid, fast-flowing waters of the Passirio River directly into the historic Old Town.

Although a base for many outdoor activities, Merano is also well known for its thermal springs which are reputed to cure rheumatism. If you are not into bathing, stroll through the Old Town with its narrow streets, numerous old buildings, and lovely fourteenth-century, bell-towered Gothic parish church San Nicolo. The fifteenth-century Landesfürstlische Castle is open to the public and is worth a short visit for the weapons and furniture exhibitions. Shoppers will enjoy the arcaded, shop-lined, and occasionally expensive via dei Portici, where unusual gifts may be purchased. This truly beautiful town situated in a most lovely valley is a walker's paradise and would make an excellent base for many mountain excursions.

Optional Maps: Kompass #53 Meran/Merano (1:50,000) or any of the other locally sold topographical maps.

Time/Distance: 1 hour 40 minutes/5 miles (8.5 kilometers).

Difficulties: Some climbing out of Algund.

Toilet Facilities: At cafés and restaurants in both towns and a public lavatory on the Tappeiner Weg.

Refreshments: Numerous opportunities along the way especially on the Tappeiner Weg.

Getting There: From Merano take the #13 bus from the train station to Algund (buses to Mals also stop at Algund but not in the town center).

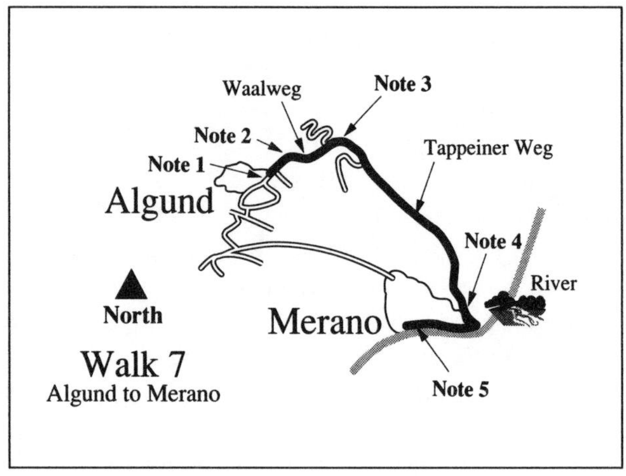

Trail Notes

___ 1a. If you take the #13 bus to Algund, walk back a couple of minutes in the direction that the bus came from until you pass a bakery; look to your left where you will see a sign indicating "Waalweg." (If you take the Mals bus, walk back in the direction that the bus came for a couple of minutes to the first left, where you will see a city center sign and a tourist information sign. Walk up this street [via Peter Thalguter] towards the church steeple which almost dead ends at the bakery mentioned above.)

___ 1b. Turn left on this vine-covered path, continuing to the top where you will ignore the possibility of turning right or left and continue to ascend. From this point you will begin to see the "Waalweg" signs, which you will continue to follow.

___ 2a. When you come to a dead end, turn right where the sign indicates "Waalweg Gratsch."

___ 2b. Just after you make the right mentioned in 2a, you will come to a fork: bear to your right and under the grape vines; do not go left and up.

___ 2c. Watch to your left for the "Waalweg" sign that takes you behind the hotel/restaurant.

___ 3a. When you reach a vehicular road, just continue downhill (on the vehicular road) in the direction of Merano.

___ 3b. After about five minutes you will see a sign indicating "Tappeiner Weg" which you will follow until you reach a large, foliage-covered entrance which also bears the "Tappeiner Weg" sign.

___ 4a. When you come to a castle keep, look to your left: there will be a little refreshment stand where you will descend on a path into town.

___ 4b. Just continue to follow the path that skirts the river all the way into Merano. Do not cross to the other side of the river.

___ 5. Turn right on the via Rezia (Ratiastrasse) in order to return to the train station.

Suggestions for More Walking

There are numerous fine walks in the area of Merano. Purchase the map recommended above or any other local topographic map for details. Of particular interest and beauty are the walks that follow the river banks to the north. You could take a bus up to Riffian and walk back, or walk up one side of the river and return on the other side.

Walk 8: Dolomites

***Walk*: Ortisei (St. Ulrich) to St. Christina**

60 mins.
3.3 miles (5.3 km)

General Description

The Dolomites epitomize the Alpine stereotype of jagged grey peaks standing tall against menacing

grey skies; however, on a clear day, golden rays piercing blue skies illuminate the peaks, bathing them in a soft glow that produces a lofty haven of tranquillity. In either case, with or without sun, the Dolomites offer some of the finest and most impressive walking in Europe.

Nestled peacefully in a deep valley and encroached upon by a magnificent coniferous forest, Ortisei exudes traditional mountain charm—macho mountaineers amble about in throngs throughout the charming commercial sector, ornate chalets dot steep mountainsides, and astounding vistas are everywhere. Delight in awesome views of high mountains as you ascend in a rapidly rising cable car that drops you (figuratively) at Seceda more than 8000 feet above sea level. From Seceda, you will begin a superbly beautiful walk through Alpine meadows surrounded by serrated peaks and green slopes along a trail which is punctuated by flourishes of luminous, multicolored wild flowers. In spite of the high-mountain locale, this is a supremely civilized walk along a trail dotted with restaurants, park benches, and remote huts that can be rented for lonely, on-top-of-the-world experiences—a deservedly well travelled path with many families making the trip.

You will descend to lovely little St. Christina, another traditional mountain town built around a diminutive valley-sized city square. Enjoy the pretty church, well-stocked shops, and lively street life.

Optional Maps: Kompass #54 Bozen/Bolzano 1:50,000.

Time/Distance: 1 hour/3.3 miles (5.5 kilometers), including the walk from the cable car station to St. Christina.

Difficulties: None.

Toilet Facilities: At cafés and restaurants in both towns and along the mountain path; also at cable car stations.

Refreshments: Numerous opportunities in both towns and along the trail.

Getting There: Park your car in St. Christina. If you have enough time or there is no parking to be found in town, you can park your car in the cable car parking lot and walk down to the bus stop, where you may take the bus to Ortisei. If you are on public transportation, buses run frequently to Ortisei, where you may begin the walk and catch a bus back at St. Christina. Cable cars and funicular run continuously throughout the day except between noon and 1 p.m.

Trail Notes

__ 1a. From the bus stop in Ortisei, walk down the main street in the same direction that the bus is going.

__ 1b. Just past the tourist information office, you will see a set of signs including a yellow one that indicates "Seceda" and has a drawing of a cable car. Turn right here and continue to follow the signs.

__ 1c. the next sign you see will have a picture of a person walking;

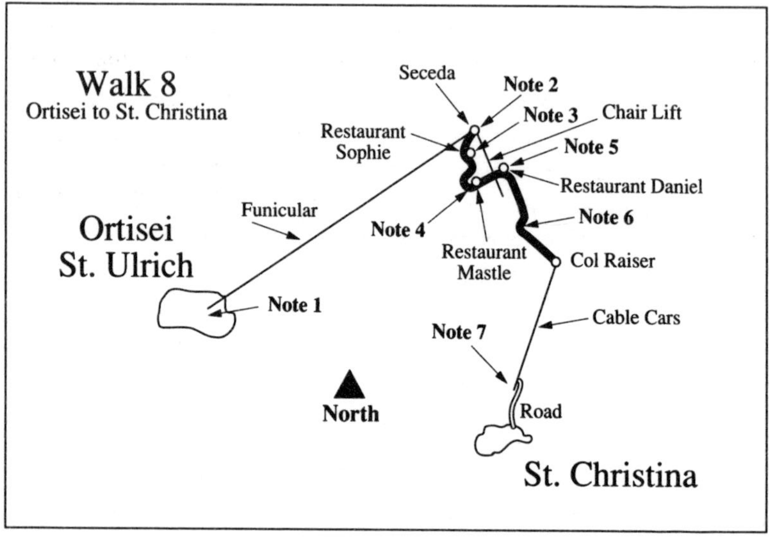

follow this to the right, ignoring the one to the left which is the car route.

__ 1d. As you ascend, a couple of minutes later you will see the funicular station straight ahead and to your right.

__ 2. As you exit the funicular at Seceda and walk behind the station, look down a wide path to the Restaurant Sophie; this is where you are going.

__ 3a. From the Restaurant Sophie, continue downhill on the wide path until you reach a dead end at another wide path, where you will go right, continuing downhill.

__ 3b. Continue to wind your way downhill to the Restaurant Mastle, which is near the chair-lift line and has a brown roof and is painted brown and white.

__ 4. From Restaurant Mastle, continue downhill and to your right to Daniel's Restaurant, which is on the other side of the chair-lift line.

__ 5. Just continue downhill from the Restaurant Daniel on the same wide path.

___ 6. As you descend, you will see the Fermeda Hutte to your right. Soon, you will see a sign indicating "Col Raiser" pointing to your left. Follow this path to the cable car station. (The cable cars leave from beneath this large structure; just jump on a cable car. You can pay at the bottom; however, no one asked me for any money.)

___ 7. From the cable car station, just walk downhill until you hit a dead end, then go right and directly into town.

Suggestions for More Walking

You may wish to combine this walk with the next walk to Selva/Wolkenstein by looking to your left as you approach the town square for the sign indicating Selva/Wolkenstein. If you decide to do this, leave your car in Selva/Wolkenstein and take the bus to St. Christina. The optional map recommended above indicates numerous walks in the valley and also high in the mountains.

Walk 9: A Valley Walk

Walk: St. Christina to Selva/Wolkenstein

50 mins.
2.5 miles (4 km)

General Description

St. Christina, embraced by arbor-covered slopes, lies recumbent and tranquil in a cool mountain valley where skiing and hiking reign supreme. Enjoy the outdoorsy ambience and stroll about the shop- and restaurant-lined city square before beginning today's amiable amble along the valley floor.

En route to Selva/Wolkenstein you will enjoy constantly changing views of the mountains; be treated to the sights and sounds of a copiously flowing white-water river and be captivated by effusive fields of shimmering wild flowers. You will also pass a charming collection of Alpine chalets and lovely, regionally designed hotels and restaurants. There is no finer way to shuttle between towns than this path, which alternates between rustic charm and sparsely inhabited resort areas. All urban areas should be designed with this sort of pedestrian traffic in mind.

Selva/Wolkenstein is another Alpine gem of a mountain town that is popular with both hikers and skiers. There are two cable cars that will whisk you above the town and into the mountains for more excursions if you should decide to spend more time in the lovely Val Gardena. Also, you may consider doing this short walk in both directions for maximum pleasure: depart St. Christina; walk to Selva/Wolkenstein for lunch; and return later sated but fit.

Optional Maps: Kompass #54 Bozen/Bolzano 1:50,000.

Time/Distance: 50 minutes/2.5 miles (4 kilometers).

Difficulties: None.

Toilet Facilities: Cafés, restaurants in both towns; occasional privacy.

Refreshments: Cafés, stores, and restaurants in both towns.

Getting There: Buses run regularly to both towns from Bolzano. If you are taking public transportation, ride to St. Christina, take the trail, and then return from Selva/Wolkenstein. If you have a car, leave it at Selva/Wolkenstein, then take the bus back to St. Christina.

Trail Notes

— 1a. From the bus stop at St. Christina, walk directly up the road, going right at the fork and looking to your right.

— 1b. When you see a sign indicating "Selva/Wolkenstein 1 hour," go to your right in the direction that it points. From this point just follow the pedestrian signs, which are blue circles surrounding the forms of a man with a little girl.

— 2a. In Selva/Wolkenstein, the trail passes behind the Sport-

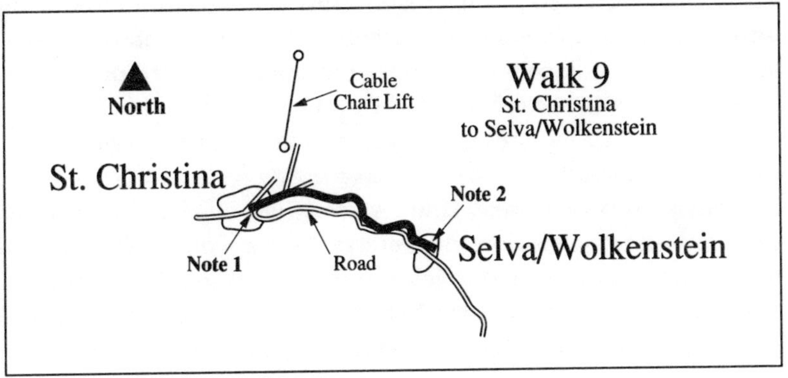

stadion Pranives Pizzeria-Restaurant. Continue straight ahead and down into town on this street.

__ 2b. When you come to a street with traffic, turn right and you will be in the town center in a couple of minutes.

Suggestions for More Walking

See the suggestions for Walk 9.

Walk 10: Lago di Garda

55 mins.
3 miles (4.8 km)

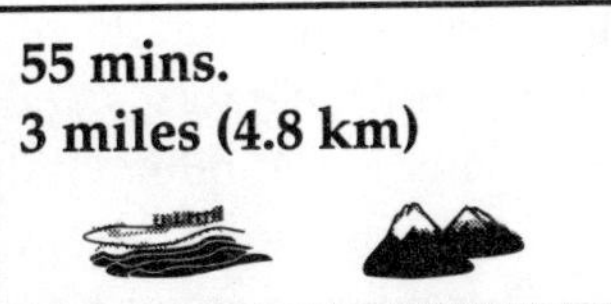

Walk: Marniga to Castelleto

General Description

Lago di Garda, largest of the Italian lakes, extends gracefully for almost 35 miles amidst an undulating landscape of verdant hills and granite cliffs which drop precipitously into the lake allowing only a thin shorehugging band of habitation, and a few communities clinging tenuously to the mountains. As daylight fades, mountain and lake conspire to produce an Olympian scene through the hazy twilight; it is not hard to imagine Jupiter himself paying an occasional visit to this lovely land. If you have time, take an automobile tour (about 100 miles) around the lake through a host of lovely lakeside resorts and along Lago di Garda's lovely banks where breathtaking views of lake and mountain are ubiquitous. During the summer, however, traffic is slow and patience is advised.

Today's walk will take you between two lovely little coastal towns, under the shadow of massive Monte Baldo. Both towns share spectacular lakeside views and a quiet holiday ambience. Marniga's charming two streets harbor a collection of shops, hotels, and restaurants catering to vacationers who seek a quiet getaway from urban clamor. As you begin the walk, ascending steeply from this tiny town, glance over your shoulder for spectacular views of lake and mountains. You will soon arrive at mysterious Campo, an eerie relic of an almost forgotten past, now hovering in the penumbra of total abandonment. (However, it is not difficult to see why this has occurred: if people had to climb this high to get to Manhattan, it would also have been abandoned long ago.)

Campo, down to its last few residents (I was fortunate enough to have seen one standing in a doorway, an elderly lady who was glad to point me in the right direction), is actually quite large, consisting of a variety of stone structures in varied states of ruin contrasting starkly with the few tidy and well-kept inhabited homes. This fascinating jumble of the quick and the dead is one of my favorite trail memories and probably itself alone worth a flight to Italy. This is definitely Italy off the beaten path.

Continuing along the trail which skirts Monte Baldo high above the shoreline, you will enjoy excellent views of Lago di Garda where the atmospheric effects are in a constant state of flux, producing a turgid, museum-worthy Impressionistic tapestry. In fact, at times you cannot see distant mountains across the lake, a visual sleight of hand imparting the impression that you are strolling along the Mediterranean coast. This stretch is a lovely wild-flowered, forested walk, sheltered by shade, and enlivened by the sonorous sounds of omnipresent songbirds. As you continue, wilderness alternates with domestication. In some places the hill has been tiered and stones meticulously placed by abundant labor in order to create *terra firma* for fertile fruit trees. The final descent from the isolated hamlet of Fazio, where events never occur, is splendid as you follow a winsome trail along crumbling stone walls in danger of losing their rocky identity to rapidly encroaching dense foliage.

Castelleto is a wider, more lively town that exploits its scenic harbor by placing several restaurants along the waterfront where there is also an inviting park, perfect for evening strolls. A number of shops and hotels also line the coastal road, making Castelleto an alluring area for a short sojourn.

If you elect to walk back to Marniga along the beach, you can stop at several places for a swim. There are, however, no broad, sandy beaches. Expect only narrow, stony strands; however, elephantine German tourists who flock here seem to enjoy them.

Optional Maps: Kompass #102 Lago di Garda/Monte Baldo.

Time/Distance: 55 minutes/3 miles (4.8 kilometers). (Add another 40 minutes if you take the beach route back to your car or hotel.)

Difficulties: 15-minute aerobic climb from Marniga to Campo.

Toilet Facilities: At cafés and restaurants in both towns; some privacy.

Refreshments: Cafés, stores, restaurants in both towns.

Getting There: Garda can be reached from Verona via bus, and buses run regularly (at least every hour) to both Marniga and Castelleto from Garda (Azienda Provinciale Trasporti Verona: tel. 800 41 29). If you are driving, leave your car at Castelleto and take the bus back to Marniga. (This is a good trail to make into a circle route, since the two towns are less than two miles apart on the main road. You could walk along the beach from Castelleto enjoying the wonderful coastal views [with only a couple minutes of road walking] to Marniga and then follow the directions in the trail notes for the return to Castelleto.)

Trail Notes

__ 1a. From the bus stop at Marniga, walk back down the main road in the direction that the bus came from looking for the Nike Hotel. (You may also walk along the beach, rejoining the road when you reach the campground.)

__ 1b. Just before you reach the Nike Hotel, turn left on the secondary road going uphill near the little bar.

__ 1c. Pass the first narrow road going up and to your right, and then go up the second narrower road to your right.

__ 2a. When you reach the top, follow the red and white waymarks (you will also see a green arrow) to your right in the direction of Castelleto.

__ 2b. When you come to the first fork, continue to follow the red and white waymarks which take you left and up to Campo (ignoring the green arrows).

__ 3a. When you reach Campo, you will follow the waymarks to the right in the direction of Castelleto and not straight ahead.

__ 3b. When you come to a second set of signs, turn right, continuing the trail indicated as "31."

__ 4. When you come to a fork, just before arriving at an asphalt vehicular road, go to the left and up, ignoring the path to the right that descends.

__ 5a. When you come to an asphalt road and human habitation you are in Fazio; follow the vehicular road as it winds downhill, looking to your right for a steeply descending path.

__ 5b. When you see the steeply descending path to your right, join it as it goes downhill (if you are not in the mood for a steep descent, stay on the road which also goes into town).

__ 6. When you reach the road again, go to your right and you will soon be in town where you will continue to descend until you reach the main road. When you reach the main road, the bus stop is to your right.

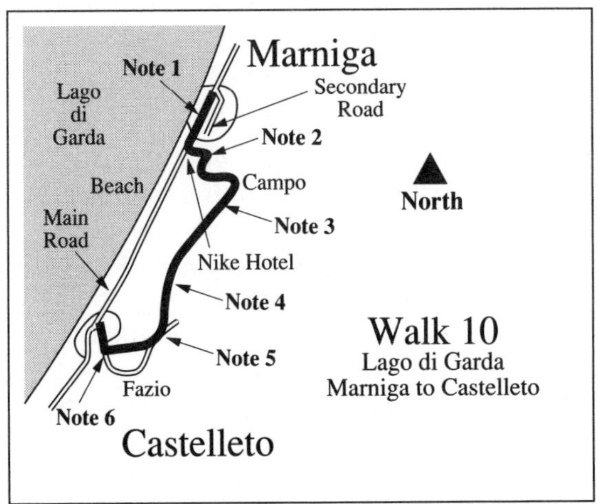

Suggestions for More Walking

Indefatigable walkers can extend this walk by taking trail #34 up Monte Baldo and eventually joining the cable cars that go even further and connect you with numerous trails high on the mountain. Purchase the recommended map for further details. Also, it is possible to walk for miles along the beaches with only occasional detours along the road all the way back to Malcesine or several miles south of Castelletto. This means you can get off the bus just about anywhere and enjoy a beach walk back to your starting point.

Walk 11: Rimini

120 mins.
6 miles (9.6 km)

***Walk*: Beach/Town walk**

General Description

What Coney Island used to be to America or what Blackpool is to the English, Rimini is to the Italians;

and, like those wonderful places, you will see muscle shirts and tattoos everywhere and on both sexes. This beach potato's Mecca is truly a unique experience—the epitome of excess in a nation of excess—cacophanaus clamor, dazzling lights, miles of sandy beach, brilliant sunlight, and immense numbers of the highly feared Dreaded Other People in a frenzy await you in this bizarre and unique community.

From wild downtown Rimini you can take the tram six miles or less along the coast and trek back through miles of tawdry, unbridled Italiana. This is a very long beach walk that can be alternated with sections of town walking for variety. Along the coast, you will inspect more bodies (everywhere and in various states of undress) than there are grains of sand on the beach; you will also thrill to the world's largest assembly of beach chairs—at least a billion. Shifting to Rimini's main drag, miles of chaos await as you pass a curious melange of low culture, including cut-rate clothing shops, *gelati* joints, pizza parlors, pick-up bars, beach accessory emporiums, leather stores (no restraining devices), sex shops (restraining devices), small amusement parks, tennis courts (for the occasional patrician traveller), disconcerting discotheques, a Roman circus, a winding water slide, and even new- and used-book vendors.

Rimini is not totally devoid of cultural curiosities, and you may wish to tear yourself away from the beach long enough to visit the Ponte di Tiberio, a Roman bridge constructed during the first century A.D., the triumphal Arch of Augustus, and the Tempio Malatestas, which is a curious assemblage of Gothic and Renaissance elements.

Optional Maps: Any city maps of Rimini and Riccione.

Time/Distance: As long as you want but the crowds are difficult to negotiate quickly: About 6 miles (9.6 km) from the end of the tram back to Rimini's town center.

Difficulties: Eating, drinking, and shopping too much.

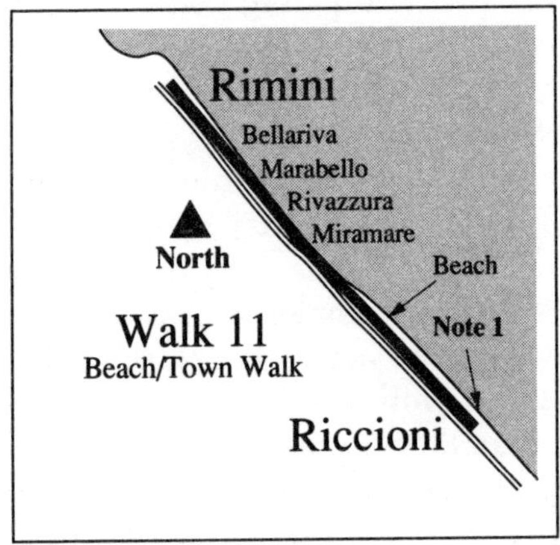

Toilet Facilities: Frequent.

Refreshments: Ubiquitous.

Getting There: Take the tram (an electric powered bus) from Rimini to Riccione or any point between. Purchase your tickets at most *tabachi* shops and validate them when you enter the tram.

Trail Notes

__ 1. Walk down to the beach and turn left. Usually there is a stone path for you to follow, but you will also have to do some sand walking. The beaches are mostly controlled by the hotels but you can enter anywhere and just keep walking. If you get tired of the beach, walk up a block and follow the rows of tacky shops for a while.

Suggestions for More Walking

You can walk down the beach and via the main road for more miles, but otherwise there are no trails in the area.

Walk 12: Florence

Walk: Fiesole to Ponte a Mensola then to Florence or Settignano

90 mins.
4.5 miles (7.2 km)

General Description

Fiesole stands tall on a hill overlooking one of the most moving sights in the world: Florence radiating radiantly along a narrow stretch of the lovely Arno River. Even though the view of Florence itself is worth the tortuous five-mile bus ride to the top of this hill, the town itself does not disappoint. Founded by the Etruscans long before there were any Romans anywhere, Fiesole provides excellent but relatively expensive accommodations and dining opportunities. In addition to the stunning multi-directional views into the land of Boccaccio's *Decameron*, there are also several outstanding tourist attractions. Most interesting is the well preserved Roman theater (with adjoining museum) built in 80 B.C., which is still used to stage plays on warm summer nights. The twelfth-century cathedral provides cool sanctuary during searing summer days and some interesting interior details. Finally, the Etruscan tombs en route to today's walk evoke many millenia-dead spirits.

Today, you will walk from Fiesole's diminutive town center along a series of narrow roads, past the Etruscan tombs, and into a world seemingly remote from urban woes but actually only a few miles from bustling Florence. Spectacular vistas abound as you stroll along rural roads and into a fragrant, deep-green, coniferous forest which bestows shady tranquillity upon overheated walkers. This ethereal forest walk is enhanced by the presence of superb wild flowers, and views of distant Tuscan hills. Along the way, you will also pass Castel di Poggio and Castel di Vincigliata (neither open to the public), which lend an air of aristocratic respectability to this otherwise rural obscurity.

Approaching Ponte a Mensola, you will enter a clearing and

pass into an orchard; be prepared to be knocked flat by overpowering views of Florence and its signature Duomo to your right and inspiring views of Settignano, another hill-top haven, to your left.

Florence, probably the finest repository of Renaissance art and architecture in the world, has been the subject of numerous books and is extensively covered in any general European or Italian travel guide. A comprehensive overview of the sights encompassed by the boundaries of this world-class tourist destination is not possible within the context of this slim volume; however, a top five list would include the unique multi-colored marble, domed Cathedral of Santa Maria del Fiore, the Uffizi Museum, which houses an astonishing array of artistic masterpieces, the jeweler-lined, fourteenth-century Ponte Vecchio which spans the Arno River, the Galleria del Accademia, home of Michelangelo's *David*, and the cavernous, fifteenth-century Pitti Palace which houses a variety of museums and sumptuously appointed living quarters. Caution: cultural overload is a distinct possibility; the overwhelming cultural encounter engendered by the Florence experience has resulted in numerous tourists joining the ranks of the "Florentine fainters" who are swooned into unconsciousness by the power of great art.

The general urban ambience is also a major attraction: dine sumptuously on fine, reasonably priced Tuscan cuisine; squander laboriously earned hard currency at shops selling high-quality/ high-priced merchandise; browse abundantly-stocked bookstores (books in English are commonly available); and stroll along narrow lanes which evoke the ghosts of Renaissance past.

Optional Maps: Kompass #660 Firenze—Chianti.

Time/Distance: 1 hour 30 minutes to Ponte a Mensola/4.5 miles (7.2 kilometers) and an extra 30 minutes to Settignano or an extra hour to Florence.

Difficulties: Some minor climbing.

Toilet Facilities: Only at cafés or restaurants in Fiesole.

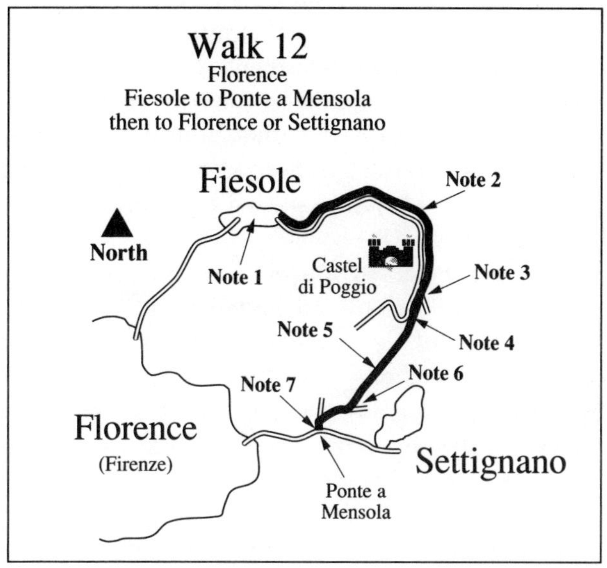

Refreshments: At Fiesole, Florence, and Settignano.

Getting There: From Florence, take the number 7 bus to Fiesole. Purchase a 24-hour ticket at a machine or *tabachi* so that you will not have trouble getting a ticket for the way back from Ponte a Mensola or Settignano.

Trail Notes

__ 1a. When you exit the bus at the town square, look uphill for the equestrian statues depicting the meeting of Garibaldi and Vittorio Emmanuel. Just follow that street up past the statues (you are to the left of the parking lot). This street becomes via Gramsci.

__ 1b. When you come to the sign indicating "Tomba Etrusca" (Etruscan tombs) you may walk down for a visit, but you must continue straight along the road that you have been walking on in order to get to the trail.

___ 1c. When you come to a dead end, go left where you see among other signs one indicating "Settignano." Continue along this road and you will soon enter a pine forest.

___ 2. About 20 minutes into the walk, just past the Club Ippico, you will come to a sign that indicates "Vintigliata" and "Settignano": turn right here and continue along this road, where you will begin to see red and white waymarks which you will follow.

___ 3. After having passed Castel di Poggio, you will come to a fork where you will go to the right in the direction of Vintigliata and *not* in the direction of Settignano.

___ 4. As the road makes a tight turn, continue to follow the red and white waymarks, leaving the road and entering the forest (in the beginning, the waymarks have a number "2" painted over them).

___ 5. When you come to a very large house, walk around it to your right and continue the trail on the other side of it (do not walk all the way around the house, just continue as if a straight line were drawn through the house) where you will begin to see waymarks again. (It would be more convenient to walk straight through the house but the owners would probably object.) After you pass the house just keep descending while watching carefully for the waymarks.

___ 6. When you come to a narrow, asphalt road go to the right, still following the waymarks.

___ 7. When you reach a main road at Ponte a Mensola (there is a little bridge over a mostly dry river here) you have three options:
a. Turn right and go to the bus stop to take one of the frequent buses back to Florence (either bus will take you there, and make sure you have purchased your 24-hour ticket in advance).
b. Go left and walk about 30 minutes into scenic Settignano and take the bus back to Florence.
c. Turn right and walk about an hour into Florence which is mostly boring until you begin to enter the city center.

Suggestions for More Walking

There are a number of walks in the general vicinity of Florence and they can be seen on the recommended optional map. Also, you may wish to visit the travel bookstore Libreria il Viaggio at Borgo Degli Albizi 41/r 50122 Firenze (tel. 055-240489), which has numerous books and maps for Tuscany and the rest of Italy.

Walk 13: Siena

60 mins.
3.2 miles (5.1 km)

Walk: Monteaperto to Siena

General Description

Although there is nothing beyond a bus stop and a couple of buildings at Monteaperto, you will be stunned by the views of distant Siena rising majestically from the fertile Tuscan plain. Although this walk takes you along an infrequently travelled rural road, it is the only route that will take you on foot into Siena, a city you will not want to miss. This pleasant and interesting stroll along a frequently shady, narrow band of asphalt (the only distraction being an occasional car) takes you through rolling fields punctuated by a couple of sleepy hamlets. The slow pedestrian pace provides you with an opportunity for a glimpse into the lives of ordinary people who live on the fringes of Sienese culture.

At the walk's completion, you will enter the walls through an impressive medieval gate, Porta Rispini, and enjoy one of Italy's finest cities. Abundantly endowed with art treasures and architectural masterpieces, Siena merits more than the day trip from Florence that is usually rationed in a whirlwind tour. The massive, semi-circular Piazza del Campo is the center of Sienese life and venue for the annual medieval procession and horse race known as the Palio delle Contrade. The cyclopean, thirteenth-century town hall and adjacent structures that line the Piazza del Campo make this one of the most attractive squares in Italy and a unique locale for imbibing both beverages and medieval history. The stunning (with its red, white, and black marble facade), world-class, thirteenth-century cathedral is also not to be missed. A variety of museums and palazzi add to the charm of tortuous alleys and sonorous street life, completing a super sojourn in this medieval Mecca.

Optional Maps: Kompass #661 Siena—Chianti/Colline Senesi.

Time/Distance: 1 hour/3.2 miles (5.1 kilometers).

Difficulties: None.

Toilet Facilities: Only in Siena.

Refreshments: Only in Siena.

Getting There: From Siena, take the #22 bus to Monteaperto, which is only a couple of homes built near a bus stop. Make sure to buy your ticket before you enter the bus at a *tabachi* or café. Alternately, you may simply want to walk out of Siena, timing your arrival at Monteaperto to meet an incoming bus, but the views are much better walking into the city.

Trail Notes

__ 1. Just follow the road you came out on back to Siena. Do not follow the waymarks away from the road you are on. At the present time, they lead you in a confusing circle to nowhere (a situation that should be remedied in the near future).

__ 2. When you come to a stop sign go right past some stores then left around the traffic circle and follow the "Porta Rispini" and "Centro" signs into town.

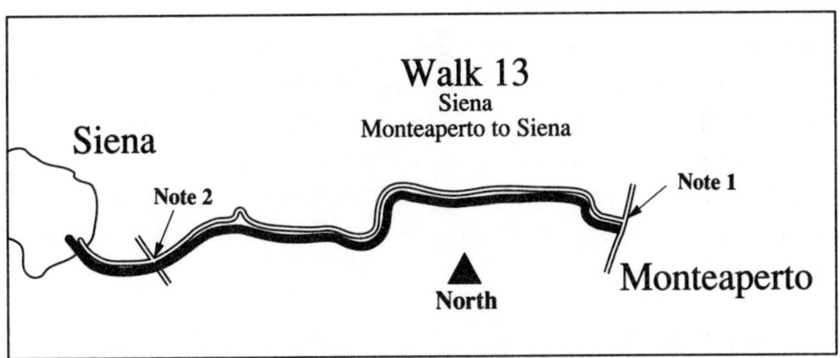

Suggestions for More Walking

Unfortunately, the area around Siena is growing rapidly and the countryside is being consumed by this "progress." Currently there are no other possibilities for a walk into Siena.

Walk 14: San Gimignano

Walk: Zona di Foci to San Gimignano

70 mins.
4 miles (6.4 km)

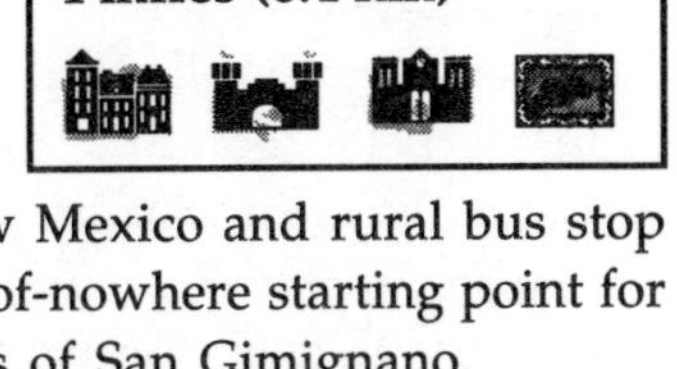

General Description

Zona di Foci, an area reminiscent of the arid hill country in northern New Mexico and rural bus stop par excellence, is your in-the-middle-of-nowhere starting point for today's high walk to the lofty towers of San Gimignano.

From the Zona you will quickly ascend a hill while gazing through vast fields at distant San Gimignano, which rises regally amidst rolling hills that stretch ad infinitum into the horizon—an astonishing sight. Watch again for excellent views of San Gimignano as you reach the vineyards and villas of the summit. Continuing to trek tranquilly along the trail, shaded by stands of fragrant

pine trees, you will enjoy an effusion of brilliant wild flowers, and be dazzled by fields of densely packed, domesticated sunflowers. Not far from the city gate, you will pass through a small village and a suburban subdivision—even the smallest Italian cities are experiencing a move to the suburbs.

San Gimignano, towered haven for financially elite travellers (the monetarily challenged can find lodging at the youth hostel or in a private room that can be booked by the tourist office), is probably the most visually stunning of the Tuscan hill towns, and not to be missed by anyone. Like many towns in Italy, San Gimignano is itself the main attraction: narrow winding streets, intimate city squares, and tall towers casting long shadows combine to make this small patch of intricate urbanity an enduring visual delight.

Strolling about this living, fourteenth-century museum (little has changed in almost six hundred years), you will feel as if transported into the European Middle Ages. The major attractions are the 14 towers (originally, there were 72), constructed as castle keeps that dominate San Gimignano's skyline. Feuding political factions would seek tower shelter during times of trouble. Climb to the top of the tallest tower, Torre Grossa, which looms 180 feet above the Palazzo del Popolo; amble along alleys to the Piazza del Duomo for a visit to the fourteenth-century cathedral; climb to the fortified Rocca for a visit to the ruined castle; and view the fine Renaissance paintings on display at the municipal museum. There is no finer way to experience Tuscany.

Optional Maps: Kompass #660 Firenze—Chianti.

Time/Distance: 1 hour 10 minutes/4 miles (6.4 kilometers).

Difficulties: A 15-minute climb.

Toilet Facilities: Only at San Gimignano where there are public toilets; some privacy.

Refreshments: Only at San Gimignano.

Getting There: From San Gimignano (the bus stop that is almost directly in front of the gate is only for arriving passengers: wait at the bus stop that is next to the parking lot) take the bus that goes to Poggiobonsi which runs several times daily to an area that is called Zona di Foci. Show the driver your map since not too many people get off at this stop (it is the first stop after the fork in the road which divides to go either to Poggiobonsi or Colle di Val d'Elsa). Buy your ticket at a *tabachi* in town. If you have a car, you may want to scout the area out so you know what the area looks like when you arrive.

Trail Notes

__ 1. When you descend from the bus, walk back to the fork in the road that the bus has just passed.

__ 2. When you reach the fork, go right until you come to the first road which is marked by signs indicating "Canneta"

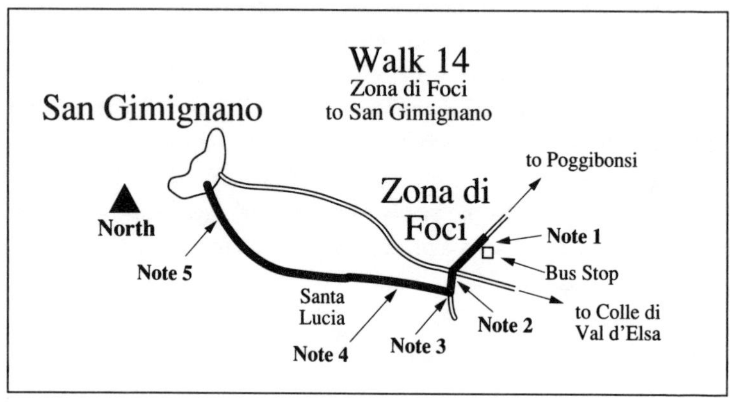

and "Podere la Colombaia." Turn left here, and walk up the hill.

___ 3. Turn right at the first gravel road, just after you have crossed a tiny bridge (there is a sign indicating "Strada Privata [private road]," but you as a walker are free to use this right of way).

___ 4. When you reach the top of the hill, you will come to a fork; go right and up avoiding the path going left and down. At this point just continue straight ahead on the path which becomes a gravel track, and finally an asphalt road.

___ 5. When you reach an intersection, just follow the signs to San Gimignano.

Suggestions for More Walking

Using the optional map suggested above, you could almost double this walk by taking a bus to Colle di Val d'Elsa and following the same trail back to San Gimignano. Another good but circular route would involve walking out of the back gate of San Gimignano and then returning to town via a series of mostly side roads. This route is also clearly indicated on the optional map.

Walk 15: Island of Elba

Walk: Monte Capanne to Marciano

105 mins.
4.5 miles (7.2 km)

General Description

Although highly commercialized and heavily frequented during summer months, Elba is large enough to absorb the crowds of tourists who flock mostly to the sandy beaches leaving the interior comfortably free of unctuous sun-worshippers. Comparable to a sun-drenched Greek island, Elba is a visual delight: miles of sandy beaches ring a mountainous interior; languid villages slumber lazily though protracted summer days; and constantly changing panoramic vistas astonish at every bend of the road. Although beaches and mountains are Elba's main attraction, there are also some interesting historical attractions here where Napoleon was exiled for about a year.

Portoferraio, today's point of disembarkation, is an attractive, sun-saturated port/beach town that serves as a good point of departure for today's adventure. If you have time, visit one of Napoleon's habitations, Villa dei Mulini, which still harbors his personal library and other vestiges of his imperial stay. Three miles from Portoferraio, in the hills at San Martino (bus #1), you may also visit Napoleon's summer home where superb views of Portoferraio and the interior mountains abound.

The inexpensive bus ride between Portoferraio and Marciano is itself worth a trip to Elba; you will enjoy an hour's tour of the island in both directions as the bus winds its way along narrow roads from panoramic vista to panoramic vista of the Mediterranean Sea, magnificent mountains, and splendid hilltop and coastal towns.

From Marciana, a cable car takes you almost to the peak of Monte Capanne. As you ascend Elba's highest mountain, you will be greeted by astonishing multi-miled vistas and will be able to survey the course of the entire walk you are about to take. From the cable car station, another few minutes on foot will take you to the summit where you can survey the breathtaking spectacle of the entire island.

The lovely descent from Elba's highest point is replete with astonishing vistas, beautiful secluded forests, and the preternatural calm of the Elban high country. You will often be able to see three towns, high mountains, and the blue sea all at once—a uniquely complex and gratifying view found nowhere else. The final approach into Marciano, through a series of narrow back streets, is truly Europe through the back door.

Spend a few moments exploring the tiny web of tangled alleys that comprise this pacific hilltown; settle into one of the comfortable cafés along the cliff-side promenade; and savor delightful views of the distant Mediterranean Sea.

Optional Maps: The most detailed map is Carta Turistica e Dei Sentieri Isola d'Elba (Edizioni Multigraphic-Firenze: 1:25,000), but other maps are commonly available.

Time/Distance: 1 hour 45 minutes/4.5 miles (7.2 kilometers).

Difficulties: An initial 30 minutes of steep downhill walking, after which the trail is easy to walk on.

Toilet Facilities: At cafés and restaurants in Marciano; café at Monte Capanne.

Refreshments: At cafés and restaurants in Marciano; café at Monte Capanne.

Getting There: It is best to get an early start for this adventure since there are a number of transportation connections involved:

1. *Ferry*: Piombino is the point of departure for ferries to Elba. Two ferry lines, Navarma (tel. (0565) 22 12 12) and Toremar (0565) 91 80 80) make the voyage to Portoferraio on Elba and their prices are virtually identical. Since they also depart from the same port,

take the one that best suits your schedule—departures are frequent. To get to the port, just follow the "Porto" signs.

2. Bus: Elba is served by ATL buses (tel. (0565) 90 42 73) which depart from the center of the port area in Portoferraio. Marciano is served by six buses per day, less on the weekend. The bus station, where you can pick up a schedule and purchase a round trip ticket, is in an office where you will see all the bus stops. Your bus is marked with "Marciano" signs.

3. Funivia (cable car): (Caution: The cable cars are basically cages that you stand in. I assume that they are safe, but if you are afraid of heights, you should close your eyes or perhaps try another walk.) The cable cars run continuously except for between 12:15 and 2:45 p.m.

Trail Notes

__ 1. From the bus stop in the center of Marciano, walk back along the road the bus arrived on until you see a right turn marked with the sign "Cabinovia," where you will board the cable car. (If you ask, the driver may let you off at this junction.)

__ 2. From where you exit the cable car, simply walk to the other side where you will see Bar la Cappanna where you can purchase refreshments. Follow the sign that indicates "Sentierio 1."

__ 3. After about 20 minutes, you will come to a promontory where you will see waymarks leading in different directions: follow the waymark that indicates "Poggio/Marciano."

__ 4. A couple of minutes later as you approach the end of the promontory, look to your left where you will continue to Marciano (do not go straight down where you see a number 2 waymark indicating "Poggio").

__ 5. Just continue on this path as it goes under the cable cars; do not go to your right until you see the red and white number 6 waymark that indicates "Marciano Pedalta."

__ 6. When you come to a dead end go to your left where the arrows point.

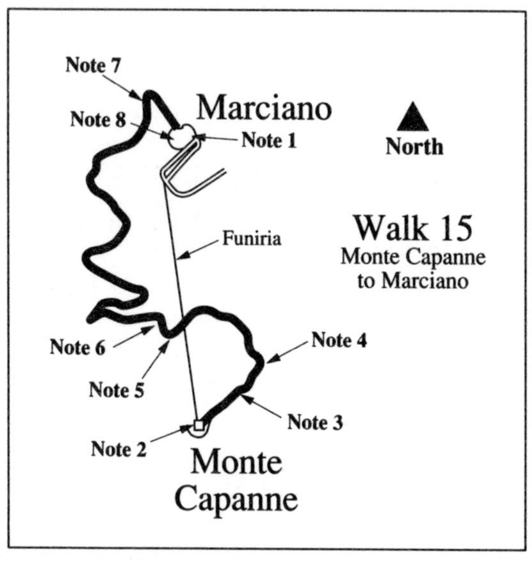

__7. Just above Marciano, when you come to an intersection, go straight ahead. Do not go left and up at either fork. Just look for the arrow that takes you down to the right.

__8. Just past the castle, look for the footpath to your right that takes you down and into the town.

Suggestions for More Walking

In order to extend this walk, you could take the bus to Poggio, climb Monte Capanne, and then follow the rest of the walk to Marciano. The walk can be shortened by following the route to Poggio from Monte Capanne. The recommended optional map indicates the paths of all of the island's marked trails.

Walk 16: Parco Naturale della Maremma

Walk: A Ramble from Marina Albarese

60 mins.
3.3 miles (5.2 km)

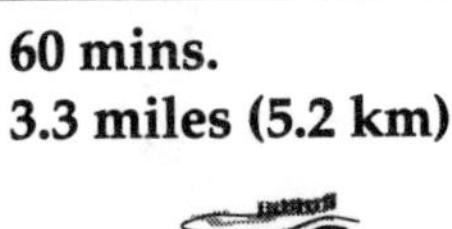

General Description

Parco Naturale della Maremma harbors the last unexploited nine miles of Tuscan coast, and it has been claimed that it is also home to the last unspoiled stretch of Mediterranean coast in all of Italy. If you can tear yourself away from the rustic tranquillity of the sandy beach long enough, this is a good place to enjoy the Mediterranean coast and get a great walk at the same time.

Today's walk begins at Marina di Albarese, where the beautiful Mediterranean is most limpid, and fragrant pines root themselves almost into the gentle blue waves of the sea. The narrow, sandy beach which requires sunbathers to cling territorially to any available patch of sand remains ungroomed and strewn with abundant amounts of driftwood. No attempt has been made to change the natural appearance of the entire area, and the only concession to humanity is a parking lot, a toilet, and a couple of refreshment stands.

Departing Marina di Albarese, you will soon be coursing through a deep-green pine forest where the cicadae sound sonorously and the trees radiate a most fragrant aroma. Emerging from the forest, you will follow the Ombrone River along a sandy bank until you reach the Mediterranean where the sound of cicadae cedes slowly to the crashing of waves driven by fresh winds. There, you will stand in awe of the river's mouth which has a barren, end-of-the-world appearance. Beside swollen sand bars, littered by a contorted assortment of gnarled driftwood, witness a fast flow of fresh water into this desolate stretch of untamed sea. From the mouth of the river, you will skirt the Mediterranean coast back to Marina di Albarese. Although you are only about 20 minutes from your starting point, the beach is usually abandoned at this point; enjoy a solitary swim and lounge leisurely in the sun far from the madding crowd. This is the utopian way to walk, swim, sunbathe, and picnic the entire day.

Optional Maps: Carta Turistica Stradale: Maremma (1:50,000).

Time/Distance: 1 hour/3.3 miles (5.2 kilometers).

Difficulties: None.

Toilet Facilities: Only at Marina di Albarese.

Refreshments: Only at Marina di Albarese.

Getting There: Once in the park, simply follow the signs to the Marina where there is a parking lot. Buses run occasionally to Albarese from Grosseto, but it is probably best to skip this walk if you are using public transportation.

Trail Notes

__ 1. From the parking lot go left and walk back down the road that you drove in on. You will see the sign indicating "Itinerario A7 Imbocce d'Ombrone."

__ 2. About six or seven minutes later you will see the same sign pointing left, where you will turn and follow a narrow asphalt, non-vehicular road.

__ 3. When you reach the Ombrone River, you will see a sign pointing left: go to the second path then turn left.

Suggestions for More Walking

Preservation efforts are serious in this park. The two most interesting trails (to San Rabano Abbey [5 hours] and the fourteenth-century towers [3 hours]) can be visited only with a guide on Wednesdays, Saturdays, and Sundays—be at the park office at

7 a.m. for the abbey tour and 8 a.m. or 4 p.m. for the towers tour. Other trails can be visited without a guide but hikers are admitted only between 8 a.m. and 10 a.m. or between 4 p.m. and 6 p.m.—the animals have a strong union here and insist on a long afternoon break. The trail suggested here is the only one that can be visited at any time without a guide.

Walk 17: Lago Trasemino

35 mins.
1.8 miles (3 km)

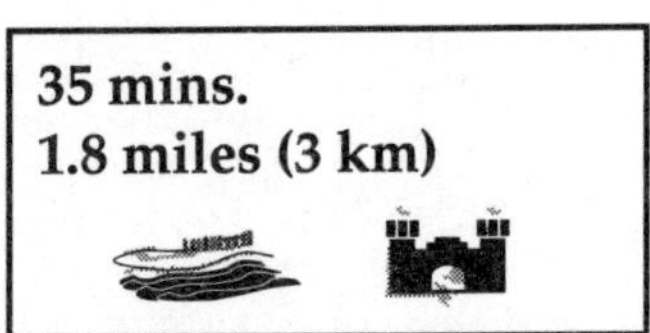

Walk: Isola Maggiore

General Description

Lago Trasemino, largest lake on the Italian peninsula and site of Hannibal's third-century B.C. rout of Roman legions, extends fluidly over 50 square miles of northern Umbria. This picturesque body of water is encircled by high hills and an uncrowded band of coastal communities that offer pleasant beaches, inexpensive accommodations, and wonderful scenery.

To begin today's adventure which unfurls upon Isola Maggiore,

largest of the lake's three islands, you must take a ferry from Passignano sul Trasimeno (shorter, more frequent, and slightly less expensive) or Castiglione del Lago (longer, slightly more expensive, but decidedly more picturesque). From walled Castiglione, Trasimeno's most attractive town (visit the fourteenth-century castle and Renaissance church Santa Maria Maddalena), the pleasurable, 30-minute boat ride brings you ever closer to the forest-green gem Isola Maggiore which rises dramatically from the emerald green waters of Lago Trasimeno. From time to time, tear your eyes from the island and look back as Castiglione and its majestic castle recede in the distance. This is a pleasure cruise you will not forget.

A painstakingly restored micro-town thrives on this mini-island. A hotel/restaurant, shops, snack bars, public toilets, and a tiny port allow Isola Maggiore's 60 residents (down from 600 in the sixteenth century) to thrive on a booming tourist industry, supplemented by fishing and crafts.

From the dock, you will embark upon the most interesting 35-

minute walk anywhere in Italy. Heading north from the town center, look to your left at the sixteenth-century church of Buon Gesu and directly next to it the fourteenth-century House of the Captain of the People. Just before departing the tiny town, note to your right the austere twelfth-century Church of San Salvatore which was restored in 1972 and is currently used for worship. Trekking from town, you will join the lovely coastal trail where there are several sandy beaches and plenty of opportunities to stop for a picnic. About midway along the eastern shore, you will encounter a statue of St. Francis of Assisi which commemorates his landing in the year 1211 for the purpose of praying and fasting during the 40 days of Lent. Just above it is a chapel that purports to contain the block of stone that served as a pallet for the saint. Near the island's southern tip is the fourteenth-century Church of Saint Francis and Monastery of the Friars Minor Observants, which were purchased by the wealthy Marquis Giacinto Gugliemi in the late nineteenth century and converted into a castle/villa. The walk back to town takes you once again along the coast and quickly back to the port.

This is a superb excursion, particularly on a sunny afternoon when you may sun, swim, and picnic the day away.

Optional Maps: Purchase the inexpensive tourist booklet *Isola Maggiore* at the tourist information booth as you exit the boat. Included is a detailed map.

Time/Distance: 35 minutes/1.8 miles (3 kilometers).

Difficulties: None.

Toilet Facilities: Public toilets near the port.

Refreshments: Restaurants and cafés in the port area.

Getting There: Ferries leave frequently from the port at Castiglione.

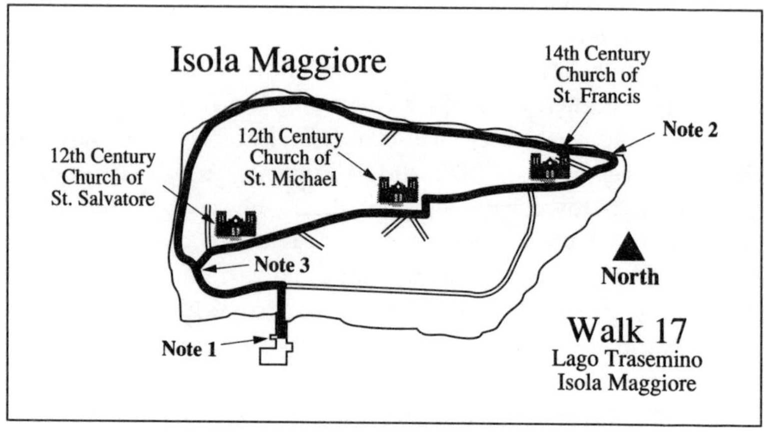

Trail Notes

__ 1. From the port, walk up to the main road and turn left continuing along the coastal path as it winds its way along the island.

__ 2. When you reach the other end of the island, go to the right and up, passing the Church of St. Francis and continuing along the path to the Church of St. Michael.

__ 3. When you pass the Church of San Salvatore, go to your left and return to the port.

Suggestions for More Walking

For extra walking, cover the island twice or perhaps swim back to Castiglione. Actually, this is a small patch of land and does not lend itself to a lot of trail modification.

Walk 18: Gubbio

Walk: Monte Ingino to Gubbio

50 mins.
2.7 miles (4.3 km)

General Description

Gubbio is a lovely red-roofed town that rises in steep terraces beneath the immensity of Monte Ingino. This relic of a bygone era strongly evokes images of the Middle Ages: stroll picturesque stone streets that harbor shops brimming with crafts (ceramics in particular are noted for quality and value); inspect medieval ramparts that enshroud Gubbio in a protective sheath that seems to repel the hordes of tourists seen at other Umbrian hill towns; and dine with epicurean arousal on tempting truffles, a regional specialty.

Once you have dined and enjoyed the genuinely medieval ambience, visit both the Consul's Palace and the Ducal Palace (both begun in the fifteenth century) and then amble out of medieval walls into the ancient world where a Roman theater built during the reign of Augustus still stands; from the top of the theater, the views of Gubbio are excellent. Finally, inveterate church-visitors will want to visit the twelfth-century cathedral and the thirteenth-century church of St. Francis.

When you are ready for a major out-of-walls experience clamber out of the Porta Romana and climb up to the cable car station for a quick rise to the top of Monte Ingino. Revel in ever-changing views of the town and valley as you steeply ascend in your own personal basket. Soaring above grey-stoned, red-roofed Gubbio you will note the stark contrast from the muted greens and golds of the rolling Umbrian landscape.

At the summit you can visit the Basilica di Sant'Ubaldo (named after Gubbio's patron saint) and continue to gaze into the distance at the rolling hills and gentle valleys of this Umbrian arcadia. Reluctantly averting your gaze from distant splendor, begin the descent into Gubbio while enjoying exceptional views of the town

and its environs. Continuing along on a downward trajectory you will pass through a forest shaded by towering pines, be delighted by a variety of multi-hued wild flowers, and encounter several chapels while savoring soothing silence punctuated only by the occasional sounds of sonorous songbirds. The final entry into Gubbio is a joyous experience as you pass through a medieval gate, encounter almost immediately the impressive cathedral, and continue along narrow cobblestone streets to the town center.

Optional Maps: Kompass #675 Sentiero Europeo E 1 Tratto Umbro (1:50,000).

Time/Distance: 50 minutes/2.7 miles (4.5 kilometers).

Difficulties: None.

Toilet Facilities: At the café on Monte Ingino and at restaurants and cafés in Gubbio.

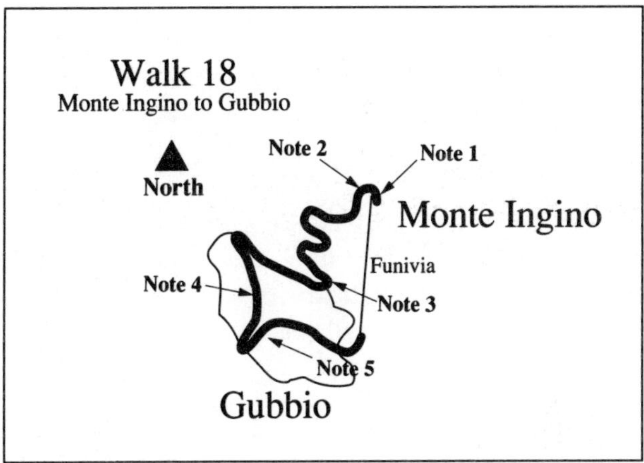

Refreshments: At the café on Monte Ingino and at restaurants and cafés in Gubbio.

Getting There: From Piazza dei Martiri where buses stop and where you will enter the town if you drive, walk up a couple of blocks (pick up a town map at the tourist office which is on the left as you are walking up) and turn right on the Corso Garibaldi, following it until you go left and out the gate where you will see signs for the *funivia* (cable car).

Trail Notes

__ 1. As you exit from the basket at the station, you will notice a path on the other side of the cable which you will take to the Basilica of St. Ubaldo.

__ 2. From the entrance of the Basilica just walk downhill on the asphalt path where you will pass through a stile which will not allow motorized traffic to enter.

__ 3. When you pass through the town gate, go to your right and down.

__ 4. When you come to a street with vehicular traffic, just continue straight and down via Mastro Giorgio (you will see a number of signs indicating various hotels, restaurants, etc.).

__ 5. When you get to Corso Garibaldi (you will see a large café with a large exterior space), turn right and continue along to the Piazza dei Martiri where you began.

Suggestions for More Walking

This walk can be extended by continuing upwards along the minor road and then descending in a circuitous *unmarked* path that eventually takes you to the outskirts of Gubbio. This path is clearly indicated on the above optional map.

Walk 19: Assisi

Walk: Eremo delle Carceri to Assisi

60 mins.
2.2 miles (3.5 km)

General Description

Assisi, a living labyrinth of medieval memorabilia, gently cascades along the slopes of immense Monte Subasio and basks in the glory of some of the finest art anywhere in the world. This pilgrimage destination par excellence will be one of your favorite Italian sojourns; and, although you will not be bereft of fellow sojourners, you will find Assisi to be comfortably accommodating and a haven of spiritual tranquillity.

St. Francis, son of a wealthy merchant, was born here in 1182 A.D. After a debaucherous youth, he founded the Franciscan Order and devoted the remainder of his life to helping the poor and talking to animals. His spiritual presence persists, and Assisi thrives on the pilgrims who continue to flock to the traces of his memory.

Assisi's most remarkable sight is the Basilica di San Francesco, which is actually two churches, one on top of the other. The lower, Romanesque structure harbors the crypt of the saint and is adorned by an extraordinary collection of frescoes by Giotto, Cimabue, and

the Lorenzetti brothers. The upper, Gothic structure (the first Gothic church in Italy) is home to a series of 28 frescoes depicting the life of Saint Francis. Painted by Giotto and recently restored, these are perhaps the finest frescoes in the universe.

There are also several other notable churches, including the church of Santa Maria della Minerva, which was constructed during Roman times and was formerly a pagan temple devoted to Minerva; the Cathedral of San Rufino, which has a superb facade; and the Gothic church of Santa Chiara.

Other interesting sites include the fourteenth-century Rocca Maggiore, a well preserved medieval fortress above the town offering excellent views of the valley; Piazza del Comune, formerly the site of the Roman forum; and the via San Francesco which is lined by medieval and Renaissance houses. In addition to numerous sights, the city itself is superb and home to a variety of local crafts.

After a day of rapt astonishment in Assisi, you will pass through the medieval gate Porto Cappuccini and quickly enter a quiet world free of vehicular traffic—only the occasional cooing of white doves ruffles the otherwise preternatural silence. Beginning the ascent from Assisi, you will ramble along medieval walls and penetrate the forest that St. Francis knew intimately. The trail becomes progressively more precipitous, and the arduous, rocky ascent should serve as a penance for all of your past indiscretions, although perhaps not painful enough to qualify you for sainthood. However, as you ascend, multi-miled views compensate for the difficult climb; and after about 35 minutes the trail does become fairly level and presents no problem.

The Eremo delle Carceri, nestled picturesquely into Monte Subasio, appears as if it is about to be swallowed by the encroaching emerald-green forest. Saint Francis frequently climbed to this site for quiet meditation and, it is said, to preach to the birds. The lovely, fourteenth-century structures that are open for tourism were not here during Francis's lifetime, but you may visit the cave that contains the saint's rock bed and the small church, cut from rock, that was in existence when Francis visited. The densely foliaged grounds of the Eremo are illuminated by brilliant, multi-colored wild flowers and graced by swarms of colorful butterflies. You will want to pass some time exploring this place of otherworldly beauty before returning to ethereal Assisi.

Optional Maps: Kompass £663 Perugia/Deruta (1:50,000).

Time/Distance: 1 hour uphill/50 minutes downhill (2.2 miles each way).

Difficulties: If you decide to go both ways the first 35 minutes uphill will burst your lungs—go slowly.

Toilet Facilities: Public restrooms at Assisi and Eremo delle Carceri; some privacy.

Refreshments: Cafés and restaurants in Assisi; refreshment stand at Eremo delle Carceri.

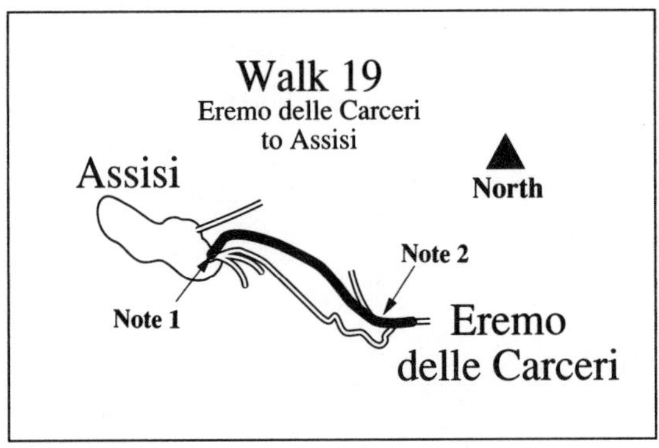

Getting There: There is no public transportation to Eremo delle Carceri, but taxis from Assisi will transport you quickly up the hill where you can visit the Eremo and return on foot. If you are in the mood for an aerobic workout, walk both ways.

Trail Notes

__ 1a. From Place Matteotti in Assisi, where there is a parking lot and bus stop, walk north to where the road forks and go right following the sign that indicates "Eremo delle Carceri."

__ 1b. When you pass through the gate, go left along the path which is marked with a red and white waymark and the numbers 50 and 51. You will not have trouble finding the trail from this point.

__ 2. When you reach the traffic road, just go right. You will see a red and white waymark.

If you took a taxi to the top, do the following: From the parking lot, walk up the asphalt traffic road, following it until it curves right. Look to your left, after about eight minutes, where you will see the red and white waymark. Turn left here, and walk down the narrow path to the left of the picnic tables. The trail will take you right into Assisi.

Suggestions for More Walking

For an all-day death march, continue uphill from Eremo delle Carceri (watching for the number 50 waymarks) to Monte Subiaso and then down to Spello where you can catch a bus back to Assisi. Other trails appear on the recommended optional map and I am told the trails in this area are fairly well marked.

Walk 20: Spoleto

60 mins.
3.2 miles (5.1 km)

Walk: Monteluco to Spoleto

General Description

Spoleto, not far from Assisi and one of the most impressively situated Umbrian hill towns, tumbles gracefully down a heavily forested hill and almost into a deep ravine. This lovely site is covered by a medieval labyrinth of narrow streets, narrower alleyways, and petite plazas where you may repose at a café or wander aimlessly about while browsing curious shops that harbor sundry crafts, memorable trinkets, and just plain rubbish disguised as souvenirs.

As you amble about Spoleto, take time to tour the Piazza del Duomo, which is lined by magnificent palaces and crowned by a twelfth-century, Romanesque cathedral. Inside, you will marvel at a series of rose windows and also several frescoes by Fra Filippo Lippi (who died just before completing the frescoes and continues to reside, entombed, in the cathedral). From the cathedral, climb to the Rocca, a well preserved fortress that looms over the city and provides excellent views of town and countryside. Just beyond the Rocca and spanning the deep ravine of the Tessino River is the Ponte delle Torri, a fourteenth-century aqueduct, built on a foundation dating from Roman times, which is now a pedestrian link between Monteluco and Spoleto. Also notable is the church of San Salvatore, which is one of the oldest in Italy, dating back to the fourth century but modified in the ninth century; inside, note the Corinthian and Ionic columns dating from Roman times. Other Roman memorabilia include the Triumphal Arch of Drusus (23 A.D.), a Roman theater, a first-century home recently uncovered, and an archaeological museum.

When you have exhausted the numerous sites at your disposal but are not yet yourself exhausted, take the bus to Monteluco, a lovely high-country haven of tranquillity. Here, in this quiet and unspoiled village, close to bustling Spoleto, you will long linger over lovely views of Spoleto and its formidable castle. From Monteluco, you will begin a continuous downhill trek through a deep, quiet forest which thins from time to time, providing excellent views of Spoleto and the surrounding countryside. Leaving a series of switchbacks behind, you will then traverse the Ponte delle Torri, wend your way beyond the formidable Rocca, and penetrate Spoleto through a medieval daedal of intricately woven passageways.

Optional Maps: Be certain to have a city map, which you can get for free at the tourist office; a city guide which can be purchased at newsstands also includes a map—without a city map your return through this medieval labyrinth could be slowed by about a decade. The tourist office also has a free topographical map "Spoleto: Guida dei Sentieri e Passeggiate con Cartina Topografica," which indicates this trail and several others.

Time/Distance: 1 hour/3.2 miles to the town center; add an extra 10 minutes to the train station.

Difficulties: None.

Toilet Facilities: At restaurants and cafés in Spoleto; little privacy.

Refreshments: Refreshment stand and restaurant in Monteluco; at restaurants and cafés in Spoleto.

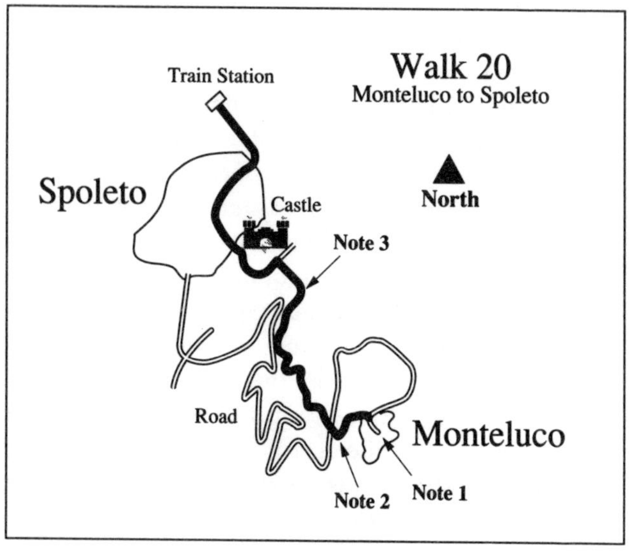

Getting There: Buses to Monteluco depart seven times daily from the train station, Piazza Garibaldi, and Piazza Carducci. If you have arrived by automobile, it is best to park and take the bus from the train station since there is virtually no parking available in the city; this involves about 10 minutes of extra walking.

Trail Notes

__ 1a. Walk back a couple of minutes on the road that the bus arrived on. You will see a souvenir stand and a refreshment stand and, just behind, a small church.

__ 1b. Just before you reach the church, you will see a path where you will turn to the right and which will take you past a small hotel.

__ 1c. When you reach the hotel, you will see a path to the left which you will follow downhill. You will also see a red and white waymark with a number 1, which indicates the trail you will be following into Spoleto.

__ 1d. When you come to the first fork, go left.

__ 2. When you come to an asphalt road, go briefly to your right while you look to the left for the waymark that will take you down the trail almost immediately. (The following section of the trail is quite clear but remember to keep going downhill at any fork.)

__ 3. After you cross the bridge leading to the castle, go left and follow the asphalt road as it winds around. There is no good way to describe a route through this maze, so you must try to make your way to the Piazza Garibaldi where you can pass through a gate and into Piazza della Vittoria and continue to the third street, viale Trento e Trieste, where you will turn left and walk to the train station. (Do not follow the traffic signs that lead to the train station, since these are for vehicular traffic and will take you far out of your way.) Use your city map.

Suggestions for More Walking

This walk can be expanded by walking both up and down the hill or by following this same trail (which is actually a large circular trail) in the opposite direction as it winds its way back to Spoleto. From Monteluco, it is also possible to join several of the other trails indicated on the tourist office map.

Walk 21: Mediterranean Pines

75 mins.
4 miles (6.4 km)

***Walk*: Silvi Marina to Pineto**

General Description

Silvi Marina and Pineto are basically quiet beach towns without the neon pretensions or frenetic pace of Rimini. Both, however, are crowded with Italians during July and August. However, again, if you are cruising up or down Italy's east coast either town will provide an excellent sojourn, and the beach walk is great.

This walk will take you along an unusually attractive stretch of the Abruzzi coast and you will follow a beautiful, sandy beach the entire way. Wear your sandals or even go barefoot as you skirt the coastal waves; you can stop for swimming and sunning almost anywhere you desire. However, this is not just another pretty beach walk; traversing this very narrow strip of level land between hill and sea, you will have excellent views of the hills and towns in the distance. As an added bonus, one of the finest stretches of coastal pines in Italy parallels the beach. Fragrant and peculiarly bent by coastal winds, this strip of verdant pines harbors a lovely trail that you may walk along if you can tear yourself away from the sandy beach.

As you approach Pineto, you will pass a painstakingly restored defensive tower known as the Torre Cerrano that is now used as a marine biology laboratory. Soon you will be in central Pineto, where you may shop or imbibe at the tourist stores, cafés, and bars that line the main street and city square. If you have time, take a quick, six-mile drive up the hill to Atri for a more relaxed hill-town atmosphere where you will enjoy good food, a couple of Renaissance churches, and expansive views of the surrounding countryside.

Optional Maps: I have been told that there are no topographical maps that cover this area (except the outdated IGM maps); however, there is absolutely no necessity for a map on this trail.

Time/Distance: 1 hour 15 minutes/4 miles (6.4 kilometers).

Difficulties: None.

Toilet Facilities: At both train stations and at various cafés along the way; no privacy.

Refreshments: Restaurants and cafés in both towns and at various points along the walk.

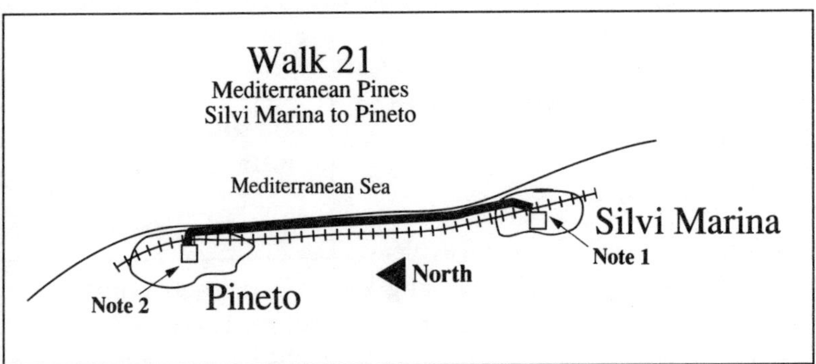

Getting There: From the train station at Pineto, take the train to the first stop south, Silvi Marina. Trains run at least 20 times daily. Wait for the train at track number 3.

Trail Notes

___ 1. When you arrive at Silvi Marina, go to the underpass and turn right onto a street that will take you almost immediately to the beach where you will turn left and procede to walk back to Pineto.

___ 2. As you enter Pineto, begin to look to your left for the train station (it is obscured by trees but visible), where you will find an underground passage to the town.

Suggestions for More Walking

I was unable to find any more trails in the vicinity and the tourist office personnel could think of none either.

Walk 22: A Walk on the Wild Side

100 mins.
5 miles (8 km)

Walk: Stazione Porto di Vasto to Lido di Casalbordino

General Description

Stazione Porto di Vasto is a bleak, modernesque train station serving a vast industrial complex that appears to threaten a hazardous contents spill into the Mediterranean Sea. However, the sea is clear and beautiful here, indicating no disaster has yet occurred. From Stazione Porto di Vasto, the initial passage to the sea is not conventionally picturesque, but it is nevertheless an interesting and unusual excursion as you pass through a surrealistic, deep-shadowed industrial zone (one of the many that are rising in menacing ugliness in otherwise beautiful areas of Italy) that harbors factories, warehouses, pollution, etc. Passing quickly without transition from the industrial zone to agricultural fields is unsettling, and you may wish to ponder the future of Italy's coastal heritage at this point.

You will reach the Mediterranean at the Punta Aderci, which projects sharply into the sea and provides award-winning views in all directions. Here the sea is perfectly pellucid—emerald greens flow quickly into azure blues and the sea floor guards no secrets from peering eyes. From the Punta, you will descend to an almost abandoned stony beach that attracts few frolickers because only local inhabitants know the maze of dirt roads that allow access.

About midway, there is a long, impressive expanse of massive boulders that you will have to negotiate (or you could wait around for a couple of billion years for the boulders, to erode into a sandy beach). There is usually a path behind the boulders but from time to time you must scramble over them in order to complete the walk. At the end of this long expanse of boulders, you will come upon a group of cyclopean concrete pylons that are easy to walk upon, but again, watch your step. The final approach to

Casalbordino includes a walk amidst pines along a former rail line, a scenic bridge crossing, and a return to the now sandy beach.

Casalbordino marks a return to civilization, although perhaps not a complete return since it is debatable whether Italian beach culture qualifies as true civilization. In any case, Casalbordino is an attractive, fairly quiet beach town with an excellent beach that is pleasing for an overnight stay.

Optional Maps: None except the IGM map.

Time Distance: 1 hour 40 minutes/5 miles (8 kilometers).

Difficulties: This is a more adventurous trek since you will not be close to traffic for most of the walk, and there is a stretch of beach strewn by boulders that can be, at times, difficult to negotiate (do not undertake this walk in the rain). Although there is a narrow path behind most of the boulders, you will have to do some minor climbing; be very careful and wear hiking boots.

Toilet Facilities: At both train stations; much privacy.

Refreshments: Restaurants and cafés at Lido di Casalbordino.

Getting There: Take the train from the station at Casalbordino to the Stazione Porto di Vasto, which is the next stop. There are six trains daily—take the train in the direction of Foggia or Tamorli. Currently you cannot purchase a ticket at the station in Casalbordino—you are advised to purchase it on the train.

Trail Notes

__ 1a. When you arrive at Stazione Porto di Vasto cross over the tracks to the little station which you will pass and go left on the road that leads to the station.

__ 1b. When you reach another road in a couple of minutes, turn right.

__ 1c. Turn right in another couple of minutes where you see a sign indicating "Porto." Continue to walk straight along this road, past the traffic circle, and towards the sea.

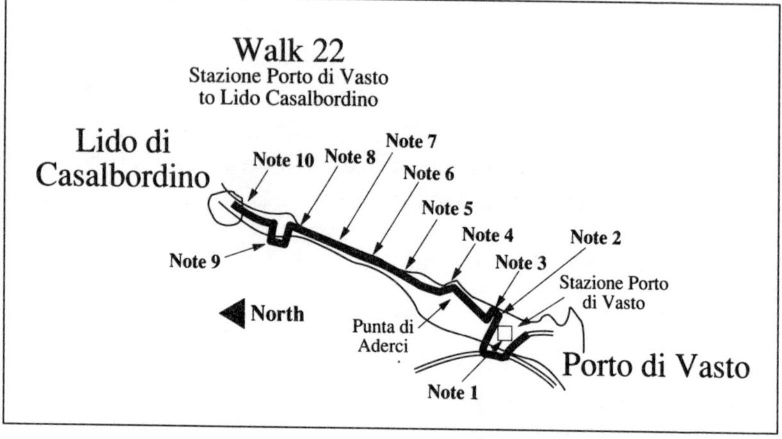

— 2. When you reach a dead end, go left along a road that parallels the sea where you see a sign indicating "Punta Aderci."

— 3. When you come to the first intersecting road, look to your left, and you will see another "Punta Aderci" sign which leads you along a dirt path down to the sea.

— 4. From Punta Aderci, follow the dirt path down to the beach.

— 5. When you reach a beach filled with boulders, simply follow the narrow path behind the boulders; you will occasionally need to climb over some boulders in order to make your way.

— 6. At the end of a long expanse of boulders, you will come upon a group of concrete pylons that are easy to walk upon, but again, watch your step.

— 7a. When you come to the end of the concrete pylons, look to your left for a narrow, grassy trail leading upwards.

— 7b. Turn right quickly on the path just before the stone fence and continue to follow the trail above the beach which is a former rail line.

— 8. When you come to a fork, stay left along the brick wall which will lead you to a bridge that you must cross.

___ 9. After you cross the bridge, you will reach a point where you can go left or right; go right and follow the road around until it reaches the beach where you will turn left and walk into town.

___ 10. When you see the restaurant Stella del Sud (surrounded by numerous international flags), go to the left where there is an underground passage leading to the train station.

Suggestions for More Walking

There are no marked trails in the general vicinity, and beach walking is not always possible given the rocky nature of the local beaches.

Walk 23: Ancient Rome: Caput Mundi

Walk: A Walk Along the Via Appia Antica into the Center of the Ancient Universe

160 mins.
8 miles (13 km)

General Description

Rome, formerly center of the ancient universe and now center of modern Italy, is at or near the top of any short list of not-to-be-missed cities in the world. You could spend weeks rambling about ruins, hopping from church to basilica to cathedral, and inspecting more museums than most cities have homes. However, if you do not have time for a protracted visit, a short stay would certainly require a visit to the Roman Forum and the numerous other associated ancient monuments at the city center, Saint Peter's Basilica, and the Vatican museums which harbor many of the world's greatest art treasures. For a longer stay, you will want to purchase the Michelin green guide to Rome which is comprehensive, concise, and clearly written, or any of the other numerous guides to Rome.

Today's walk spans one of the world's great archaeological

treasures, the Via Appia Antica. This venerable road was opened in 312 B.C. and followed a serpentine course all the way to Brindisi on the Adriatic Sea. As a result of a law that banned burials within the city, numerous tombs were located along the route, and the three-mile tomb-walk from Casale Rotondo (where you first join the Appian Way) to Cecilia Metella's tomb includes many of the most interesting and spectacular of these ancient burial monuments.

Departing from the Casale Rotondo, an immense cylindrical tomb dating from the Republican era, look to your left for an excellent view of an impressive but crumbling aqueduct. You will then traverse this great-stoned ancient thoroughfare and be awed by the remains of tomb after tomb after tomb which line both sides of this remarkable band of exterior museum. Ambling beneath the tall, shady pines that line this ancient route, you will occasionally come upon flowing fountains that supply cool drinking water to the weary traveller; drink heartily, and anoint yourself if you are hot. Just behind the tombs of the ancient nobility are the villas of the most wealthy of modern Romans—peer through monumental gates, and regard enviously the expansive grounds and impressive abodes of the rich and famous.

When you arrive at Cecilia Metella's tomb, pause for a brief inspection of this Republican-era monument which was converted to a fortress during the Middle Ages. Just beyond, you will encounter the tomb of Romulus, son of Maxentius, an early-fourth century emperor, and the remains of a hippodrome that Maxentius had erected for chariot races.

Soon you will reach a series of catacombs (St. Sebastian, Domitilla, and St. Callistus), which are part of a vast network of subterranean galleries dating back to the third century A.D. that were used for Christian burials and worship. You can be guided through these hoary monuments to early Christian devotion and determination by assiduously efficient friars before your return to Rome.

The walk from the catacombs to Porto San Sebastiano is safe but noisy because of traffic volume. You may wish to take the bus up to the city walls and then continue on foot into the center of Rome, trekking like a Roman past the Baths of Caracalla, the Circus Maximus, the Coliseum, and directly into the great monuments of the Roman Forum. A dazzling assemblage of stellar sights from beginning to end, this is truly one of the most historically significant walks in the world.

Optional Maps: Many maps of Rome extend far enough to cover this walk.

Time/Distance: 2 hours 40 minutes/8 miles (13 kilometers).

Difficulties: From the catacombs to the gate Porto di San Sebastiano there is a fair amount of traffic which can be avoided if you take the bus back to the Porto di San Sebastiano from the catacombs.

Toilet Facilities: Train station at Torricola; at the café near the catacombs; cafés and restaurants in Rome; some privacy.

Refreshments: Café at the catacombs, numerous opportunities in Rome, and expensive restaurants in the vicinity of the catacombs.

Getting There: From the main train station in Rome (Stazione Termini), take the train which is marked "Nettuno" from platform (*binario*) 14 to the first stop at Stazione Torricola. Trains run approximately every 60 minutes, and schedules are posted around the station. You can purchase a ticket at one of the crowded windows or theoretically at one of the ticket machines (which function in English) around the station. I had no luck at the machine, nor have I ever come out ahead on a slot machine—you may be more fortunate.

Trail Notes

Attention: Bring a city map to aid your navigation when you have entered the city walls.

__ 1. As you exit from the station at Torricola, take the asphalt road that goes to the right.

__ 2. When you come to the next road in about five minutes, turn right again.

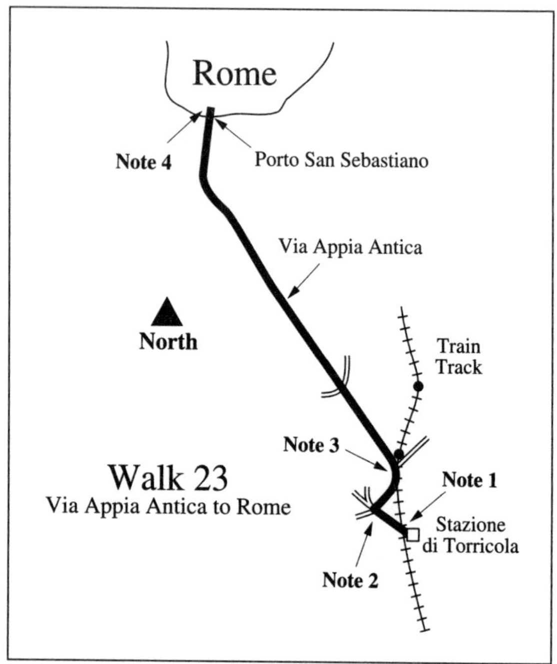

— 3. When you arrive at another intersecting road, go left; you will be on the Via Appia Antica, and there will be a sign indicating your location—follow this road all the way back to Porto San Sebastiano in Rome.

— 4. As you enter the city, continue to follow the via San Sebastioni which takes you to the Baths of Caracalla and then follow the signs to the "Coliseo" (coliseum) and visit the nearby Roman Forum before making your way back to the train station with your map of Rome.

Suggestions for More Walking

You can shorten this walk by about one half by taking the bus to the center of Rome from the catacombs. Also, there are numerous, informative books that describe walks within Rome in a variety of languages. However, there is no carless way to access the city from beyond the walls.

Walk 24: Tivoli/Hadrian's Villa

130 mins.
5.4 miles (8.6 km)

Walk: San Polo de Cavalieri to Tivoli

General Description

San Polo de Cavalieri is a wonderfully quiet hilltown typical of this lovely region and a good place to stop for a snack or beverage before heading down to Tivoli. Lots of people gravitate to Piazza Marconi and idle away the hours at the café or on one of the numerous benches where you may enjoy distant views. After you experience San Polo and before you embark upon today's adventure, stop at the ornate fountain conspicuously located in the Piazza Marconi in order to fill your water bottles with the cool, pure drinking water that flows so freely.

As you trek from town, continue to look over your shoulder for excellent views of San Polo as it slowly diminishes in the distance: you will see a comely collection of weathered abodes flowing fluidly down a gently sloping green hill. As San Polo fades from view, you will hike quietly to the sound of cicadae along a superb crest with million-dollar views of valleys, hills, and towns. The excellent and ever-changing views of Tivoli and the plain which seem to stretch in infinite vastness are available only to the walker. Leaving forest and field behind, you will arrive at Tivoli, a favorite vacation spot among ancient glitterati, superbly situated in the Sabine hills just 20 miles from Rome. Illustrious visitors included the Emperor Augustus, Maecenas, the great patron of the arts, and Hadrian, who built the great villa that still astonishes late-twentieth century visitors.

Tivoli is still a pleasant enough location to draw harried Romans from their urban morass to a day in the country. The town, a winsome tangle of short streets and surrounding broad boulevards, can be quickly explored on foot. Two great villas demand a pause for close inspection. Surrounded by some of the finest gardens and fountains in Italy, the sixteenth-century Villa d'Este is a masterpiece of Renaissance architecture. The Villa Gregoriana, attractively situated along the banks of the Aniene River, also beckons town wanderers with its quiet but rather untamed grounds which are dominated by the precipitously raging, 300-foot Great Waterfall. Located high across the river from Villa Gregoriana are two ancient temples dedicated to the Vesta and the Sybil where you will enjoy impressive views of the villa's grounds and Tivoli. There is also a Roman amphitheater, a cathedral constructed between the twelfth and fifteenth centuries, and numerous other worthy sights to distract you from walking. In fact, if you are not wrapped in a stringent temporal straightjacket, a visit to Tivoli can merit two days.

Finally, located three miles from Tivoli is one of Italy's most renowned tourist attractions, the sprawling Villa Adriana (Hadrian's Villa). Designed by the Emperor Hadrian during the early years of the first century A.D., this estate is an astonishing testimony to the wealth and power of Rome at its apogee. Hadrian, a well travelled student of art and architecture, attempted to recreate some of the most impressive sites of the empire, and the vast grounds envelope a variety of unique structures, including an imperial palace, a maritime theater, and several baths and libraries—all built to serve the great emperor's needs.

Optional Maps: Unfortunately, beyond the dated IGM map, there is no suitable map for this walk. However, there is no problem navigating until the very end when Tivoli is in sight.

Time/Distance: 2 hours 10 minutes/5.4 miles (8.6 kilometers).

Difficulties: The final approach into Tivoli can be confusing since a malevolent farmer has plowed a very large field and destroyed the waymarks in the process. However, you are within sight of Tivoli at this point and the directions provided in the trail notes should be adequate for finding your way into Tivoli. You will also need to pass through several gates which you are free to open and then shut. They are simple wire and wood structures that can be opened by pulling a wire loop from the top of the gate and sometimes unravelling other wires. It is very advisable to wear hiking boots on this trail.

Toilet Facilities: None between towns, but much privacy.

Refreshments: At bars, restaurants, and cafés in both towns.

Getting There: From the bus station at Tivoli (not far from the train station) take one of the eight daily buses (six on Sundays and holidays) to San Polo de Cavalieri. Buy your tickets before boarding the bus at the station. If you are carless, you may also take a bus from Tivoli's bus station to Hadrian's Villa.

Trail Notes

__ 1a. The bus will drop you in the center of this diminutive town, and you will walk back down the road from the bus stop very briefly to the Piazza Marconi, a small square where you will see a café, a few other businesses, and a fountain with cool drinking water.

__ 1b. From Piazza Marconi, head downhill along via Roma, the same road the bus took into town.

__ 1c. A minute or two later, when you reach a fork, go to the right and away from the road that the bus arrived on.

__ 1d. When you reach a second fork, a couple of minutes later, go right again where you see a large blue "P" (for parking) sign.

__ 1e. When you reach a third fork in another couple of minutes, go left and descend on a narrow asphalt road. Here you will see a red and yellow waymark on a telephone pole. (You should arrive at this point in about four or five

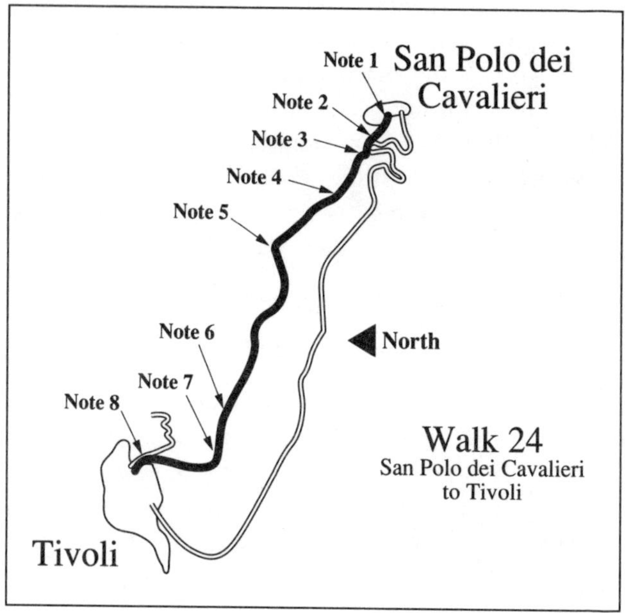

minutes.) Continue to follow this road as it changes from asphalt to concrete to gravel and dirt.

___ 2. When you reach the main road, go to your right and continue to follow it around until another waymark leads you down and to your right in a couple of minutes.

___ 3. In less than 20 minutes from the walk's beginning, you will reach a point where you can go straight and up, or right and level, or left and down. Go straight and up; you will soon see a waymark to the right on a wall.

___ 4a. After you pass through the second gate (the first gate presents no problems), go to the left at a fork. You will soon see a waymark on a tree.

___ 4b. At the third gate, you will have to slither under the wire because the farmer has it so tightly tethered. Ignore the little trail to the left and you will see straight ahead a fork

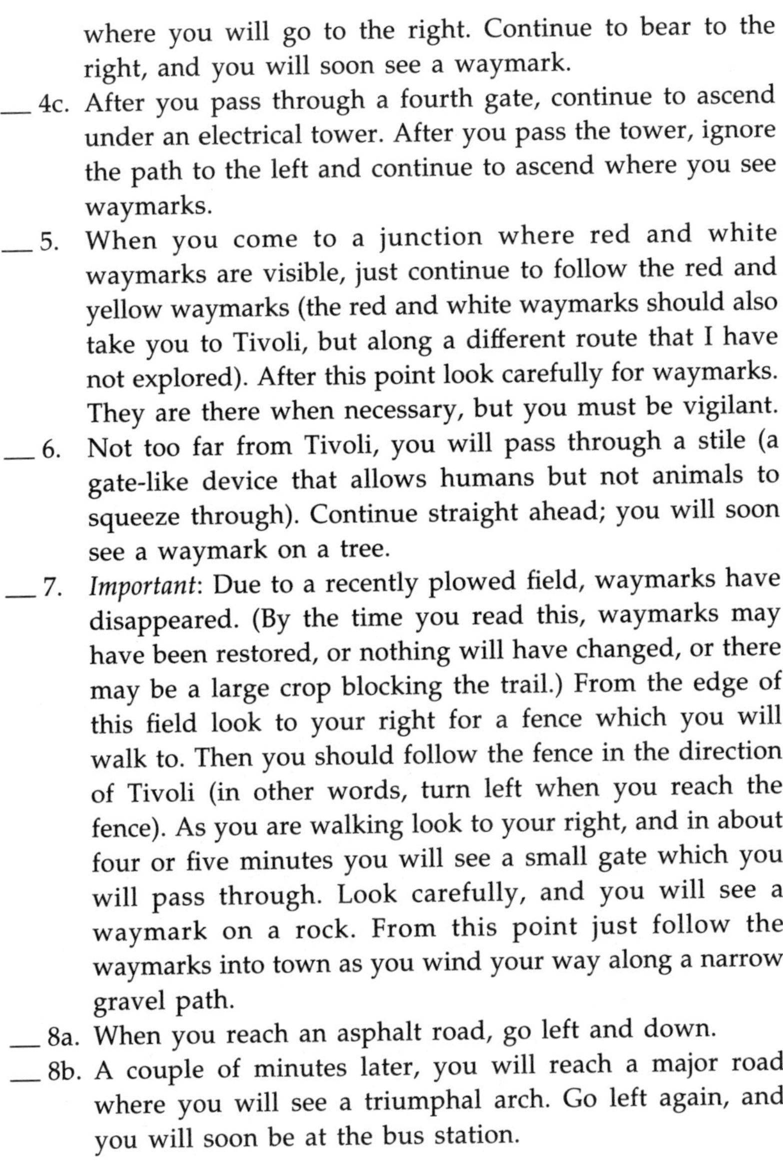

where you will go to the right. Continue to bear to the right, and you will soon see a waymark.

___ 4c. After you pass through a fourth gate, continue to ascend under an electrical tower. After you pass the tower, ignore the path to the left and continue to ascend where you see waymarks.

___ 5. When you come to a junction where red and white waymarks are visible, just continue to follow the red and yellow waymarks (the red and white waymarks should also take you to Tivoli, but along a different route that I have not explored). After this point look carefully for waymarks. They are there when necessary, but you must be vigilant.

___ 6. Not too far from Tivoli, you will pass through a stile (a gate-like device that allows humans but not animals to squeeze through). Continue straight ahead; you will soon see a waymark on a tree.

___ 7. *Important*: Due to a recently plowed field, waymarks have disappeared. (By the time you read this, waymarks may have been restored, or nothing will have changed, or there may be a large crop blocking the trail.) From the edge of this field look to your right for a fence which you will walk to. Then you should follow the fence in the direction of Tivoli (in other words, turn left when you reach the fence). As you are walking look to your right, and in about four or five minutes you will see a small gate which you will pass through. Look carefully, and you will see a waymark on a rock. From this point just follow the waymarks into town as you wind your way along a narrow gravel path.

___ 8a. When you reach an asphalt road, go left and down.

___ 8b. A couple of minutes later, you will reach a major road where you will see a triumphal arch. Go left again, and you will soon be at the bus station.

Walk 25: Caserta

Walk: A Walk from Palazzo Reggia

50 mins.
2.4 miles (4 km)

General Description

Caserta is basically a one-sight town, but the single sight is superb, and a stop here will serve as an interesting break on the way to the south of Italy or Sicily. Although modern Caserta is an uninteresting stretch of drably uniform urbanism, the eighteenth-century palace and grounds are among the great European royal residencies. Construction of the palace began in 1752 for Charles III, Bourbon king of Naples and Sicily. Designed to rival Louis XIV's great French folly at Versailles, the royal palace at Caserta (known as the Reggia) is a study in regal ostentation. This royal enormity contains 1200 rooms, 34 staircases, and enough museum-worthy masterpieces of art and furniture to pry open even the most museum-weary eyes. A tour of the royal apartments will introduce you to the lifestyles of the eighteenth-century rich and famous; the other 1100 and some rooms are not open to the public, but the *pièce de résistance* is on the exterior of the palace—the extensive grounds which, elsewhere in Europe, find no rival.

Climbing imperiously skyward in regal splendor, the 250-acre palace grounds extend royally for two miles. The grounds are so extensive that buses are necessary to shuttle weary walkers to or from the culminating cascade at park's end. However, if you are in no hurry, the four-mile round trip provides excellent and ever-changing views of the palace, the cascade, and all points of interest in the intervening space.

Departing from the palace, you will spy faintly in the distance a towering waterfall that becomes more clear with your every advancing step. However, you must tear your eyes away from this monumental masterpiece in order to survey the seven fountains and twelve little waterfalls that grace your path. The most practical of the fountains is known as the Fountain of the Dolphins, where three large dolphins spew forth a torrent of water into what is known as the Large Fishpond. Fish still inhabit this pond but are no longer bred to be eaten as they were in the eighteenth century. The Fountain of Venus, a superb collection of nymphs, cupids, and animals in magnificent motion, depicts the goddess trying to dissuade her lover Adonis from participating in a hunt that will result in his death. Expanding on the theme of the hunt, the final fountain portrays in two-part sequence Actaeon's death at the jaws of his own hunting dogs as punishment for having surreptitiously gazed upon the nude goddess Diana as she bathed. Passing the Fountain of Diana and Actaeon, you will climb high to the restful sound of water cascading over rock and arrive at a lofty height overlooking the waterfall where distant vistas of the park, palace, and surrounding countryside astonish the worthy viewer.

Optional Maps: Maps are available in the guide books sold everywhere.

Time/Distance: One way: 50 minutes/2.4 miles (4 kilometers).

Difficulties: A short but steep climb at the end.

Toilet Facilities: At various points on the grounds; no privacy.

Refreshments: Snack bar near the park boundary.

Getting There: Basically a walk up the waterfall with the option of taking the bus back or walking back from the end.

Trail Notes

___ 1. The trail begins from the palace. Simply walk straight up to the waterfall. If you prefer, you can take the bus up to the base of the waterfall and walk back. Also, you may wish to include some of the paths through the forest.

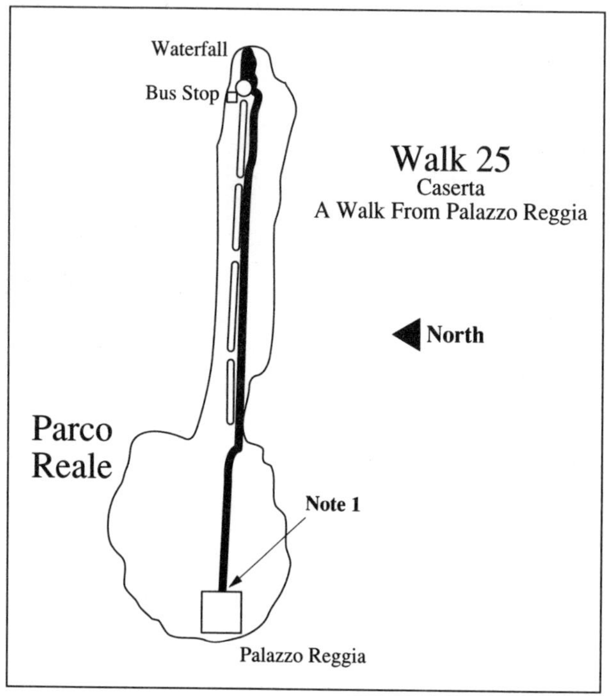

Suggestions for More Walking

This island of green is the only walk in an area of general urban sprawl.

Walk 26: Capri: Tiberius's Pleasure Island

70 mins.
3.5 miles (5.6 km)

***Walk*: Grotta Azzurra (Blue Grotto) to Capri**

General Description

The Isle of Capri has captivated visitors since Roman times. The Emperor Augustus visited several times and the Emperor Tiberius spent the final years of his life here engaged in a variety of sexual indiscretions. Today, you may enjoy this tiny, six-mile-long party island in true Roman fashion—most contemporary visitors bake by day along narrow strands of sand and revel by night in one of the many discos and clubs that abound around the island. However, if the thought of mingling, day and night, with hordes of international revellers does not excite you, Capri is easily enjoyed as a day trip from Naples, Salerno, Sorrento, or Amalfi.

Today's island hop includes all of the major sights, which during the summer are frequently too frequented, but also takes you way off the beaten Capri path and introduces you to the quiet, seldom-seen side of this island paradise.

Disembarking from the hydrofoil, you will be almost immediately whisked to the Grotta Azzurra (blue grotto) via motorboat. Dumped from motorboat to rowboat, you will float frantically (accompanied by the wailings of a so-called singing oarsman) through a small opening into a shimmering sea cavern where refracted light is bent blue with astonishing brilliance.

Having been passed from hydrofoil to motorboat to rowboat, you will rejoice as you become once again land-bound. Climbing on wobbly legs from the dock, you will soon encounter a restaurant where you may dine or imbibe while gazing into the azure-blue sea. Soon you will trek from the sea and enter a world that is seen by few visitors to Capri. You will clamber high along a seldom-used trail that affords excellent views of the Mediterranean and then enter the lovely town of Anacapri through a series of back alleys known only to the locals. The center of Anacapri is a sleepy whitewashed jumble of shops, homes, restaurants, and bars that resembles a Greek fishing village. Much more tranquil than the city of Capri, Anacapri invites you to shop, eat, or perhaps take the chair-lift to the summit of Monte Solaro where you will marvel at magnificent views of the entire island of Capri, the Bay of Naples, and points far beyond.

After about ten minutes of unpleasant road walking from Anacapri, you will again join the trail at the small church of San Antonio and begin a steep descent into the city of Capri along an almost infinite set of stairs known as the Scala Fenicia. The final approach takes you along a series of back alleys until you reach the port area known as Marina Grande. From the port you may walk up to the town of Capri or take the less leg-punishing funicular to the top. Crowded Capri, the town, is an interesting and attractive maze of narrow streets and passageways. While in town, enjoy the views, shops, and restaurants; you will also want to visit the fourteenth-century Carthusian Monastery of Saint James and the radiant Gardens of Augustus. Finally, approximately 40 minutes on foot from town lies Tiberius's palace, known as Villa Jovis, where you may climb about the ruins and enjoy excellent views of the sea.

Optional Maps: Kompass #681 Isola di Capri (1:7500) or other locally available maps.

Time/Distance: 1 hour 10 minutes/3.5 miles (5.6 kilometers).

Difficulties: What had been the established trail from Anacapri to Capri (viale Axel Munthe, just off the Piazza Vittoria) has been efficiently blocked as it makes a sharp descent because of rock slides. This results in the necessity of about ten minutes of road walking along the main road. Also, another section has been mildly blocked—meaning that the trail is still easily accessible and in my opinion, without apparent danger. If these circumstances disturb you, you may take a bus from Anacapri to Capri. However, I am content to have completed this walk all the way into Capri. Also, there is a 15-minute, pulse quickening climb from the Grotta Azzurra to Anacapri.

Toilet Facilities: At cafés and restaurants at the Grotta Azzurra, Anacapri, and Capri; some privacy.

Refreshments: At cafés and restaurants at the Grotta Azzurra, Anacapri, and Capri.

Getting There: Boats leave from Naples, Sorrento, Amalfi, Positano, and Ischia for Capri on a regular basis. After arrival, as you walk along the dock to the city of Capri, you will see a small ticket office (Gruppo Motoscafisiti Transporto Grotta Azzurra) to your left, where you may purchase a ticket for a boat ride to the Grotta Azzurra. Once there you will have to wait for a while for one of the singing row-boaters to come and get you and take you for a tour of the Grotta Azzurra (figure another $10/£6). Be certain to tell the rowboat operator that you wish to be dropped off at the dock and not returned to the boat or you will find yourself back in the motorboat heading for Capri. Alternately, take the *funivia* to Capri, where you can take a bus to Anacapri, where you can take a bus to Grotta Azzurra.

Trail Notes

__ 1a. From the bus stop at Grotta Azzurra, walk up the road via Grotta Azzurra in the direction of Anacapri (the only direction you can go). Look to your left for a staircase that you will see in a couple of minutes. Go left here, following the staircase upwards.

__ 1b. When you reach a fork, continue straight up the hill; *do not* go left where you see a painted sign indicating "via la Selva."

__ 2a. After about ten minutes on the rocky trail, you will emerge

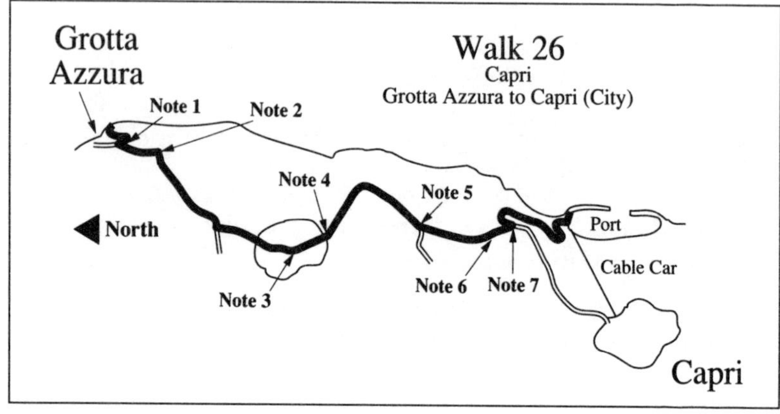

onto a narrow concrete road which you will continue to follow uphill.

__ 2b. When you come to the first fork, go left (although either way will take you into the center), and continue to make your way to the church at Anacapri's center through a maze of streets (look up to see the church).

__ 3. When you reach the Piazza A. Diaz, where the church is located, turn left along via Boffe and continue on this street until you reach Piazza Vittoria.

__ 4. (See Difficulties section above.) When you reach the Piazza Vittoria, go left along the main road via G. Orlandi as it winds around for about ten minutes (there is a sidewalk for part of the distance).

__ 5. Continue to look to your left for the Church of San Antonio, where you will leave the road and descend on a staircase. The trail at this point appears to be blocked but the metal gate that has been installed is able to be pushed open without difficulty allowing access to the descending staircase.

__ 6. Near the bottom of the stairs, there is another barrier which is easily walked around; in fact, a wooden ladder has been placed for your ease of passage (although it is not necessary).

__ 7. When you reach a traffic road, go left and follow the road around to the harbor at Capri.

Suggestions for More Walking

From the vicinity of Piazza Vittoria in Anacapri, you can take the *funivia* up to the top of Capri's highest point, Monte Solaro, and hike down. This can be done separately or as an adjunct to the walk described above. This may also serve as an excellent substitute for the walk to Capri if you have decided to take the bus from Anacapri to Capri. A number of short walks along secondary roads are indicated on the optional map recommended above; in particular, the walk to Monte Tiberio from Capri is quite pleasant.

Walk 27: Amalfi

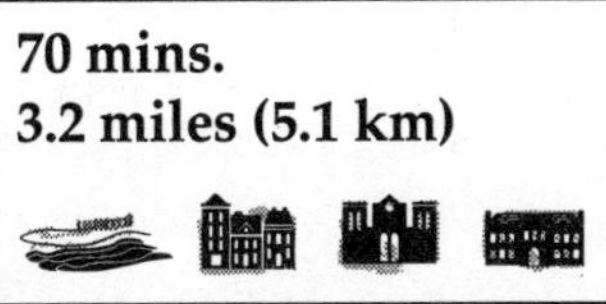

***Walk*: Ravello to Amalfi**

General Description

The approach to the town of Amalfi along a road that skirts and at times threatens to drop into the sea is one of the finest drives in the world. This stretch of the Sorrento peninsula between Sorrento and Salerno, known as the Amalfi Coast, provides nonstop panoramic dazzle. Rocky coastal mountains drop precipitously into clear blue waters; medieval towers, once a haven for Saracen pirates, perch precariously above; picturesque villages tumble tumultuously into the sea; and venerable vistas astonish with repetitive regularity.

The town of Amalfi was at one time a great maritime trading republic and a rival to Venice and Genoa. Today, international trade pretensions have disappeared but international tourism thrives. Although Amalfi is frequently bustling and occasionally bursting with tourists, it is possible to retain your sanity and find reasonably priced dining and accommodations. Amalfi's beautiful coastal site, winding, shop-lined passageways, and convenient proximity to other, less frequented towns are its main attractions, but you will also want to visit the thirteenth-century, Romanesque cathedral of Sant'Andrea, which is said to contain the remains of the Apostle Saint Andrew, the twelfth-century Cloisters of Paradise, and perhaps the town museum.

The 30-minute, tortuous bus excursion into the hills and up to Ravello is a mini-adventure in itself, generously granting excellent views and the genuine excitement of watching a variety of vehicles cautiously avoiding each other while attempting to negotiate tight turns without tumbling over steep cliffs (actually, the ride is quite safe: it just looks precarious).

Ravello, home to Gore Vidal and other literary luminaries (Greta Garbo also came here to "be alone"), can be a quiet but expensive haven for those who find Amalfi too hectic. Superbly situated on the heights above the Amalfi Coast, Ravello attracts visitors for its site rather than its sights. However, this once prosperous Renaissance town (thirteenth-century population 36,000/today's population 3000) has several worthy tourist attractions that will briefly delay your quest for the trail. The cathedral of San Pantleone, constructed during the eleventh century and later remodelled in the Baroque style, has impressive bronze doors, an ornate, thirteenth-century marble pulpit, and an attractive bishop's pulpit; the eleventh-century, Saracen-style Palazzo Rufolo has a lovely garden which the composer Wagner used as his model for Klingsor's enchanted garden; and the privately owned Villa Cimbrone allows paying visitors to visit the cloister and examine the tiles that depict the seven deadly sins.

Descending on a stone-walled staircase from Ravello, you will pass a variety of lovely old homes, some renovated and some deteriorating but all enchanting. Passing from Ravello, you will continue to descend along dirt paths and aged stone staircases while marvelling at preternatural panoramas of jagged cliffs, rugged sea, and weatherbeaten villages. You will reach the coast at Atrani, a tunnelled maze of a town worthy of a North African souk. You may wish to stop here to admire the cliff-hanging church of Santa Maria Maddelena and explore the enchanting labyrinth of homes and shops that composes this unique village. The final stage of this distinguished descent involves a passage through Atrani, a scenic trek along a cliffside path, and a steep descent along precipitous staircases into the heart of Amalfi.

Optional Maps: Kompass Map #682 Penisola Sorrentina (1:50,000) or other locally available maps.

Time/Distance: 1 hour 10 minutes/3.2 miles (5.1 kilometers).

Difficulties: Long descents on ancient stairways.

Toilet Facilities: At restaurants and cafés in Ravello, Atrani, and Amalfi; some privacy.

Refreshments: At restaurants and cafés in Ravello, Atrani, and Amalfi.

Getting There: From the harbor area in Amalfi, take one of the frequent buses to Ravello. The schedule is posted on the bar across the street from the bus stops, where you can purchase your tickets.

Trail Notes

__ 1a. From the bus stop at Ravello, you must walk through a tunnel to reach the main square.

__ 1b. When you come to the main square where the church is located, look for a sign that indicates "Villa Cimbrone"; walk in this direction, and you will soon pass under a small tunnel beneath the Hotel Rufolo.

__ 1c. As soon as you pass through the tunnel, turn left at the via Magruni and pass down a long stairway.

__ 2a. After about ten minutes you will reach a minor road where you will turn right.

__ 2b. As the road curves around, bear right, avoiding an opportunity to go left, and you will soon be walking down a very narrow concrete path which you will follow as it skirts the cliff.

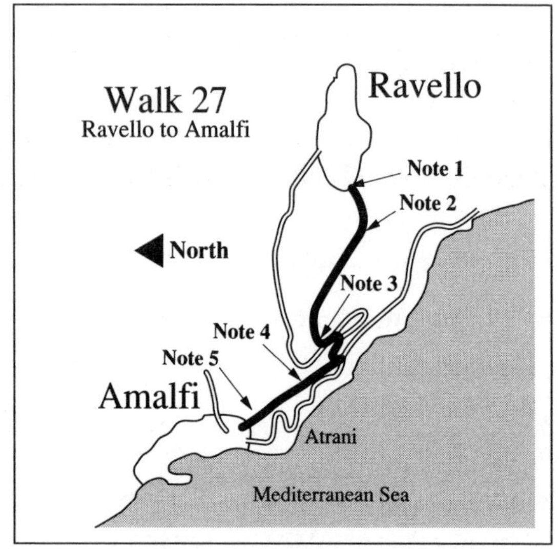

__ 2c. When you come to a fork, you will see some steep stairs going down and to your left which you will follow around until you take a sharp left and descend along a very steep stairway.

__ 3a. When you arrive at the main coast road, walk straight across and continue to descend down more stairs.

__ 3b. In a few minutes, you will reach a dead end at a house where you will turn right.

__ 4a. In Atrani, just before you reach the church Santa Maria Maddelena (you are looking at the church), look to your right for a small stairway between houses which you will follow.

__ 4b. When you see the beach to your left, do not descend; just continue straight ahead for a couple of minutes to Piazza Umberto with its drinking fountain that dispenses cool water.

__ 5a. At Piazza Umberto, continue to walk straight ahead to where you see a box for mailing letters and a sign "Supportico Marinella," where you continue straight on the very narrow covered street.

___ 5b. When you come to a dead end, go left.

___ 5c. Continue along this street as it winds right and then left until you reach via Torricelli, which you will see on your right.

___ 5d. Follow via Torricelli, and then turn left almost immediately at the first junction and follow this street as it winds into Amalfi.

Suggestions for More Walking

Numerous staircases and trails connect points in the immediate vicinity of Amalfi. Unfortunately, no one has taken the trouble of marking them. I can highly recommend a book by Julian Tippett, *Walks from Amalfi,* which describes a variety of walks from this lovely town. It is usually available from Edward Stanford Ltd. bookstore in London (tel. 0171-836-1321) mentioned earlier or from the distributor, Cordee, 3a DeMontfort Street, Leicester LE1 7HD, England.

Walk 28: Sicily: Straits of Messina

Walk: Along the Beaches North of Messina

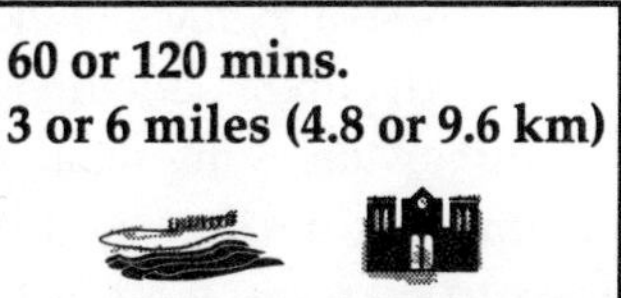

General Description

Sicily, the largest island in the Mediterranean, is only a short ferry ride from mainland Italy, but you will immediately feel the difference (especially if you have driven directly from Rome or points north): the sun burns eternally brilliant, the rhythm of life slackens, and overcoiffed Mafia hitmen prowl vigilantly awaiting new targets (actually I have never seen any Sicilian who even remotely resembled a gangster, not even in the town of Corleone—legendary home of the Godfather). In addition to providing a relaxed atmosphere, Sicily serves as a gilded repository for some of Europe's greatest historical treasures. This splendid isle has hosted such diverse groups as the Greeks, Romans, Carthaginians, Arabs, Normans, French, and Spanish. Remains of these civilizations abound, and this variegated history when combined with Sicily's superb, uncrowded beaches, scenic walks, fine food, and excellent wine produce a traveller's utopia.

Approaching Messina from the ferry, you will observe a modern city and an extensive beach that radiates north from the local docks. Messina is considered to be a drive-by on most traveller's itineraries. However, if you arrive late in the day and are in no great hurry, Messina may provide an interesting cultural experience—you will see Sicilian culture at its most candid, unadulterated by mass tourism. Although Messina was founded almost 3000 years ago, there is very little left to convey this great antiquity. A massive earthquake in 1908 destroyed over 90 percent of the town, while killing more than 60,000 people; the rebuilt Messina has an almost entirely twentieth-century appearance. Time allowing, you may wish to visit the cathedral which was rebuilt after the earthquake, the reconstructed, twelfth-century Norman church Santisimma Annunziata dei Catalani, and perhaps the Museo Nazionale, which contains a variety of treasures salvaged from the more than 100 churches destroyed in the 1908 earthquake.

I discovered today's walk one late afternoon as I arrived in Sicily. Tired of driving, I decided to stay near Messina and finally found the three-star, somewhat expensive Hotel Paradiso in Contemplazione. In need of bodily motion after a gruelling drive, I decided to take the bus up the coast road and walk back along the beach. It turned out to be an interesting look at the local beach scene, which is quite a contrast from popular, well-groomed beaches such as Rimini which draw hordes of vacationers from throughout Italy. Although this is not a superb walk, the views of the toe of the Italian Peninsula, the extensive beaches, and the Sicilian hills are excellent throughout. Finally, the intimate portrait of the lives of local beach potatoes who bake brazenly under the rays of the meridional sun is an other-worldly experience. Along this rather unkempt littoral, unsvelte and downright fat Sicilians wallow in the sand while ingesting copious amounts of fatty foods. Younger, lankier torsos frolic freely along the surf in anticipation of future fatness. Ambling along the coast while dodging often frenetic physiques, you will encounter the repulsive remains of teenagers' night fires, piles of unsightly refuse, and the tangled residue of general beach junk. If you become bored with the beach, it is possible to walk along the road which is lined with stores, cafés, and deteriorating town houses. As an added bonus, you can swim at almost any point along the walk. This is a strand way off the beaten tourist track. If you have enough time, take this trek; if you are in a hurry, go down the coast to lovely Taormina.

Optional Maps: I was unable to locate a local map, but a map is not important.

Time/Distance: 1–2 hours/3–6 miles.

Difficulties: None.

Toilet Facilities: Bars and restaurants along the way.

Refreshments: Bars and restaurants along the way.

Getting There: Just north of Messina via the #78 bus lie a number of utopian-named, non-tourist beach communities in the following order: Paradiso, Contemplazione, Pace, Grotta San Agata, and Ganzirri, which extend up to Lungo Lago (Long Lake). You may start at any point, take the bus north as far as you like (purchase your ticket at a *tabachi*), and walk back along the beach. Basically you can customize it to your own needs, since the beach stretches for about six miles between Paradiso and Lungo Lago.

Trail Notes

__ 1. From wherever you get off the bus, simply walk back in the direction of your destination.

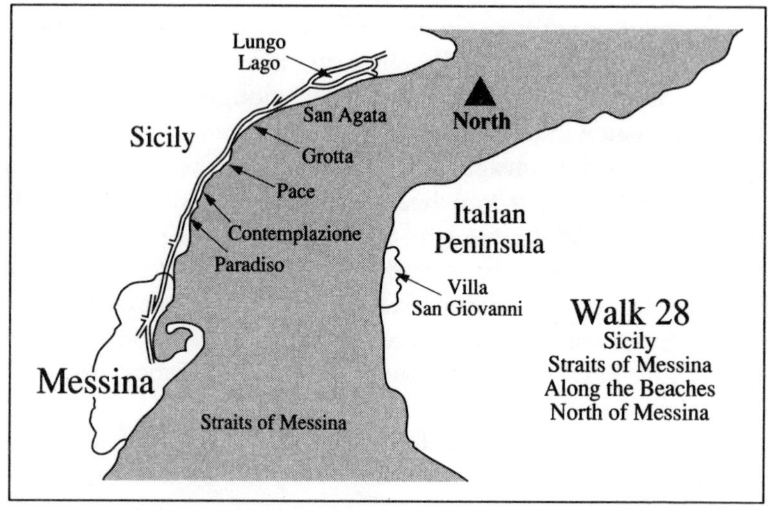

Suggestions for More Walking

No other walks here; go directly to your next stop.

Walk 29: Taormina

Walk: Giardini-Naxos to Taormina

75 mins.
3.5 miles (5.6 km)

General Description

Taormina, sublimely situated on a towering promontory overlooking the Ionian Sea, is often considered to be the most beautiful location in all of Sicily. Overawed by the distantly cast shadow of massive Mount Etna, Taormina affords admirable views in all directions and is a most charming locale to pass a rewarding Sicilian sojourn. An in-town stroll will take you through a series of pedestrian-friendly, boutique-lined streets and diminutive *piazze* that invite parched walkers to leisurely quaff cool beverages while watching local life unfold in slow motion. The restaurant scene, while not inexpensive, is studded with numerous small establishments that offer fine regional cuisine in an airy atmosphere.

The local sight-scene includes the second largest Greek theater in Sicily, a ruined castle built over the remains of the former acropolis, a fourteenth-century cathedral, the library, which was built as a church in the fifteenth century, and a lovely public garden.

Today's adventure begins with a bus ride through ramshackle Giardini-Naxos, a town that evokes a sort of Third World, perhaps Caribbean charm. Giardini's main drag is composed of an unseemly jumble of structures, mostly in disrepair, which seem ready to collapse under the weight of their own dilapidation. Shopping along the main street need not detain you, as there is little beyond local wares and tourist junk for sale. However, the beaches are superb, and night owls will hoot long into the evening and next morning around town where sound and light from numberless discos pierce darkness's otherwise nocturnal tranquillity.

Giardini has a single, excellent historic site—an archaeological zone that consists of the remains of ancient Naxos, Sicily's oldest Greek colony. Take the time to visit the digs and little museum which are along your way just before reaching the beach.

After visiting the archaeological zone, you will trace the course of the beach where you may swim at your leisure. However, at some beaches, you must pay for chair/umbrella rental, etc.; other, sometimes rockier, stretches are free, but you may have to vie for space with other sunbathers who cling tenuously to improbably rocky portions of coast, perhaps for isolation or perhaps to economize. If you tire of the beach, the many tacky stores and fast-pasta joints that line the coast road beckon you for a break. Continuing to traverse sand and stone, you will enjoy beautiful views of distant Taormina, Castelmola perched high above, and other points beyond. The final approach involves a lengthy, arduous climb to Taormina along a steep, decrepit staircase. Marvel at the multi-miled views; you will soon be back in amply amenitied Taormina.

Optional Maps: Detailed maps of both communities are available at the respective tourist offices, although additional maps should not be necessary for this walk. However, your return to a specific point in Taormina would be facilitated by the possession of a local map.

Time/Distance: 1 hour 15 minutes/3.5 miles (5.6 kilometers).

Difficulties: A 15-minute climb into Taormina at walk's end.

Toilet Facilities: Numerous bars, cafés, restaurants throughout the walk; also at the train station about midway through the walk; no privacy.

Refreshments: Numerous bars, cafés, restaurants throughout the walk.

Getting There: From Taormina's bus station (downhill on via Pirandello from downtown) take the bus marked Giardini-Naxos which runs 11 times daily to the last stop at Giardini-Naxos where the bus turns around.

Trail Notes

__ 1. From the bus stop, walk straight ahead to the first street (via Jannuzzo), turn left, and continue to walk until you reach the Zona Archeologica, where you can visit the ruins and museum.

__ 2. After about ten minutes from the bus stop (and after passing the Zona Archaeologica) you will come upon numerous signs directing you to the right, including a brown one that indicates "Spiaggia" ("beach"). Follow that street down to the sea and turn left along the beach or the sidewalk that parallels the beach.

__ 3. When the road forces you away from the beach, just follow it until you come to the first junction, where you will go right and soon be at the train station.

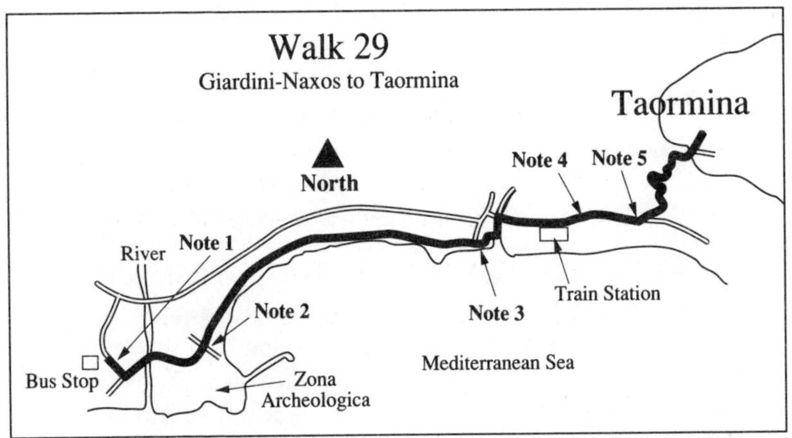

__ 4. From the train station cross the street and continue in the direction of Taormina.

__ 5. In about four or five minutes, take the first possible left turn where you see a mail box and a telephone. You will then see a "Centro" sign, where you will follow a narrow road which soon becomes a staircase leading into Taormina. When you reach the top of the hill, go left to reach the center of Taormina.

Suggestions for More Walking

Take the *funivia* down to the beaches below and enjoy a stroll along expansive, sandy strands before returning to Taormina by foot or *funivia*. Also see Walk 30 below, which can be combined with this walk for a longer distance. If you decide to walk down to Giardini-Naxos from Castelmola, combining both walks, you will go to the passageway in Taormina that has a "Hotel Monte Tauro" sign above it and continue down to the train station and then the beach.

Walk 30: Taormina

35 mins.
1.8 miles (3 km)

***Walk*: Castelmola to Taormina**

General Description

Today, after a short but tortuous bus ascent, you will visit one of the loveliest hilltop villages in Sicily, Castelmola. Poised precariously on a steep cliff directly above Taormina, Castelmola entices weary travellers with its quiet, medieval passageways which harbor charming shops, commodious cafés, and gracefully aging abodes. There is also a crumbling castle which surveys, from on high, the surrounding countryside. The descent along little-known, convoluted pathways affords admirable views of photogenic Taormina and dazzling vistas of the sea, beaches, and towns in the distance; continue to look back over your shoulder at cliff-top Castelmola for excellent and ever-changing vistas of this wonderful relic of a bygone era. You will abruptly enter Taormina along a commercial thoroughfare and proceed quickly to the center city where you will relax at a café while savoring today's visual banquet. (For a description of Taormina, see Walk 29.)

Optional Maps: The tourist office map at Taormina has a local map that includes Castelmola, but the map does not accurately depict the trail. However, the trail is not difficult to find or follow.

Time/Distance: 35 minutes/1.8 miles (3 kilometers).

Difficulties: A long descent.

Toilet Facilities: At bars and restaurants in both towns; some privacy.

Refreshments: At bars and restaurants in both towns.

Getting There: From Taormina's bus station, downhill on via Pirandello from downtown, take the bus to Castelmola which runs six times daily.

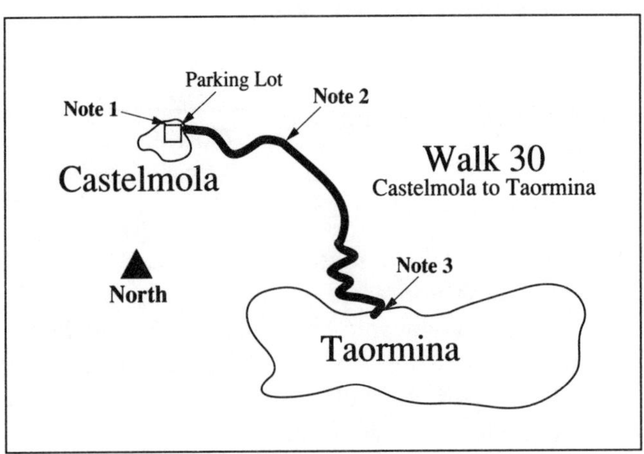

Trail Notes

__ 1a. The bus does not enter the narrow winding roads of Castelmola. From where the bus drops you, go straight up to the left of a fork and continue up to visit the city.

__ 1b. After having visited the city, descend along the same road, go right down some stairs that lead to a parking lot (the only stairs to a parking lot), and continue down on the other side of the parking lot where you follow a sign indicating "Taormina."

__ 1c. When you come to the first junction, go right and down (do not go left and up).

__ 2. When you reach the restaurant La Chioccia d'Oro, continue right and down. Look immediately left for the via Branco, which will take you into Taormina.

__ 3. When you see the "Centro" sign, follow it to the right into the center of Taormina.

Suggestions for More Walking

See Walk 29.

Walk 31: Monte Etna

Walk: Descent to the Rifugio Sapienza

70 mins.
3.1 miles (5 km)

General Description

At more than 10,000 feet, massive chop-top Monte Etna impresses not only by sheer bulk, but also by the ferocity of its volcanic activity. In recorded history well over 100 eruptions are mentioned, and as recently as 1992 the town of Randazzo, perilously placed at the base of this convoluted cone, suffered the loss of several homes under a torrent of molten lava. If you decide to peer into the crater (not required on this walk), bring an asbestos suit—several tourists plunged to a fiery death in 1979 when an unexpected tremor knocked them from the side of the rim into the caustic crater.

Today, you will take a spectacular cable car voyage 8000 feet up the side of this jet black volcano while marvelling at long views of the surrounding lava-layered landscape. This is an excellent setting for a we-are-on-another-world type of science fiction film. Exiting from the cable car, you will have the opportunity to snack, dine, or pick up a souvenir at the cable car station before sauntering downhill.

From the cable car station, the trail cuts a tortuous swathe through immense piles of lunar-looking rubble. Tons of black lava twisted into a medley of contorted shapes lie casually about the trail. Here and there brilliant patches of wild flowers cling precariously to life, defying the otherwise dormant alien landscape and demonstrating the determination of the quick to propagate even under the most exigent circumstances. In addition to the occasional, colorful floral effusion, an amazing number of shiny, happy ladybugs grace this trail—watch your step. Impressive views are everywhere; note especially the cavernous crater of Sylvestri, a partially collapsed inactive volcano which can be explored before you leave the area. As you continue to descend, vegetation increases and the contrast of earth tones on black lava forms a most inviting palette. Your ultimate at-bottom destination is the collection of tacky shops and cheap restaurants known as Rifugio Sapienza. Here you can purchase genuine Etna lava that has been carved into virtually any shape—human, animal, and unidentifiable. You can also relax on the deck of a less-than-fine-food dining establishment while imbibing both beverages and superb views.

Optional Maps: Various maps are available throughout the region, but a map is not necessary.

Time/Distance: 1 hour 10 minutes/3.1 miles (5 kilometers).

Difficulties: None.

Toilet Facilities: At both ends of the cable car; some privacy.

Refreshments: Restaurants and cafés near Rifugio Sapienza

Getting There: From the expressway E45, exit at Giarre, continuing west through Santa Venerina and following the signs "Monte Etna" and "Rifugio Sapienza." At Rifugio Sapienza take the cable car to the top.

Trail Notes

__ 1. After exiting the cable car, walk up in the direction of the ruined buildings and then turn left on the wide road which is used by the buses that ascend the mountain. Continue to follow this wide path as it winds around to your destination.

Suggestions for More Walking

From the cable car, you can take a bus almost to the summit and then make the final ascent on foot. You can also descend from this point on foot to the Rifugio Sapienza. Numerous other unmarked trails can be found on Etna and they are marked on the locally available topographical maps.

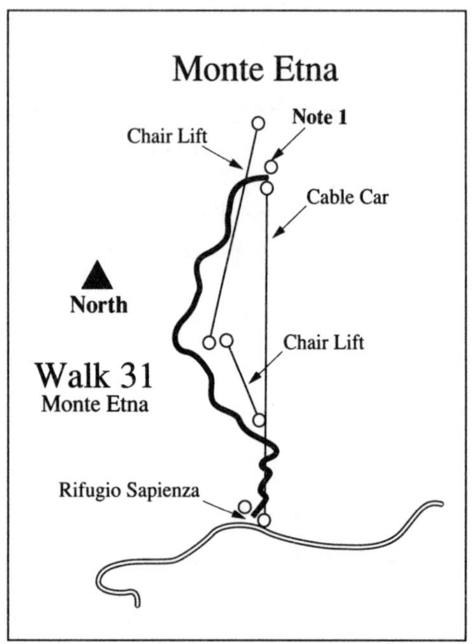

Walk 32: Agrigento

Walk: Into the Valley of the Temples

80 mins.
3.8 miles (6 km)

General Description

Beautifully situated at a commanding height amidst rolling hills of orchards and vineyards, the magnificent ancient Greek ruins of Agrigento are one of Sicily's premier tourist attractions. Founded as Akragas in 582 B.C., Agrigento boasts some of the finest Doric temples in the world. Located just south of the modern town (which served as the acropolis in ancient times), the impressive ruins known as the Valley of the Temples sprawl over a vast site and include the imposing temples of Hercules, Concord, and Jupiter, in addition to a variety of lesser ruins. Not far from the temples is the Museo Nazionale Archaeologico, which houses an interesting group of artifacts gathered from the ruins.

The city itself contains an interesting medieval quarter, and an evening stroll through narrow passageways lined with shops hawking local crafts and restaurants offering hearty home-cooked Sicilian fare is a consummate nightcap to a long and rewarding day of ancient-world sightseeing. If you have time, stop at the thirteenth-century church Santa Maria dei Greci, which was built by the Normans on the site of an ancient temple and preserves some of the ancient temple's columns. Drama aficionados will delight in a visit to the home of Luigi Pirandello, winner of the 1934 Nobel Prize and author of *Six Characters in Search of an Author*. Located not far from town (follow the traffic signs or take bus #11), Luigi's home contains a variety of the author's mementoes and is charmingly situated with excellent views of the Mediterranean Sea.

From the main square in front of the train station you will begin an interesting excursion through the newer quarters of this labyrinthine town past graffitti-covered walls and trash-covered lots into the lives of the local inhabitants. Women hang laundry across narrow corridors while shouting pleasantries to neighbors; children dash about searching successfully for mischief; and cars careen wildly along passageways almost too narrow for pedestrians. This is the real Italy, seldom seen on ordinary tours. Passing from this urban morass, you will embark upon a seldom-used dusty pathway, unfortunately pocked by incredible amounts of casually discarded trash; however, the views of the temples, the port of San Leone, and the Mediterranean Sea compensate for local unsightliness—just don't look down. This portion of the trail terminates at the museum where you may wish to investigate the engaging collection of objects found in the Valley of the Temples. From the museum it is a ten-minute stroll down a sidewalk crowded with other gawkers to the magnificent temple district where you

will stroll through temples along an ancient road that still exhibits the ruts from the many ancient carts that used to ply this busy thoroughfare. Glance up to the city of Agrigento and down to the sea; the views are excellent and this ancient encounter, found nowhere else, is superb.

Optional Maps: The tourist office has a map which indicates most of this walk.

Time/Distance: 1 hour 20 minutes/3.8 miles (6 kilometers), including a tour of the temples.

Difficulties: None.

Toilet Facilities: In town at restaurants and cafés; in the Valley of the Temples until 6 p.m.; no privacy.

Refreshments: Restaurants and cafés in town; restaurant and snack bar near the Valley.

Getting There: You will start from the train station in Agrigento.

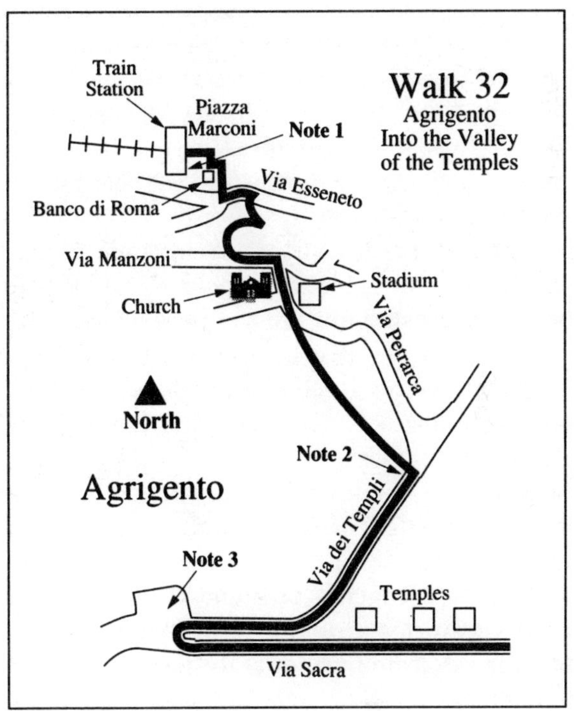

Trail Notes

__ 1a. Stand in front of the train station with your back to the doorways looking out into the parking lot where the buses stop.

__ 1b. Walk to your right until you reach a long fence almost immediately.

__ 1c. Walk along the fence away from the station until you turn quickly right down a set of five stairs, which will put you directly in front of the Banco di Roma.

__ 1d. Walk down another staircase which is next to the Banco di Roma. When you reach the bottom, you will see a sign "Salita Damareta."

__ 1e. When you reach the first cross street (via Esseneto), turn left and continue to the next stairway, where you will go right and continue to descend following it around as it goes left. Take the first right at via Niconea which you continue to follow as it winds around.

__ 1f. At the end of the via Niconea, turn left onto the via Manzoni, a major street.

__ 1g. When you come to a square in a couple of minutes, you will see the church Madonna della Divina Providenza and a small sports stadium. Go to the right where you see the arrow indicating "via Petrarca." When the via Petrarca makes a sharp left, you will see a dirt pathway descending which you will follow and have your first views of the magnificent Greek temples.

__ 2. You will meet the main road again where the museum is located. Turn right here and walk the ten minutes down to the temples.

__ 3. To return to Agrigento, take any of the yellow buses back to town from the entrance to the Valley of the Temples. Purchase tickets in town or at the bar across the street from the temples.

Suggestions for More Walking

According to the tourist office, there are no trails in this area, and recent building has obliterated secondary roads and paths that previously led to the sea.

Walk 33: Riservo di Zingaro (Palermo)

Walk: Along the Mediterranean Coast

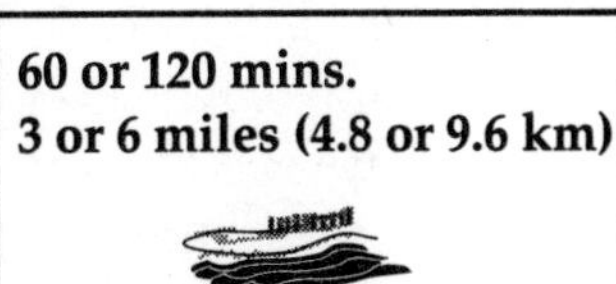
60 or 120 mins.
3 or 6 miles (4.8 or 9.6 km)

General Description

Not far from the concrete and chaos of Palermo lies a unique area dedicated to the preservation of natural beauty. This land now known as Riservo di Zingaro almost saw its destruction under tons of concrete in 1980 as part of an ill-conceived project to create a coastal road in the area. Mass demonstrations forced the abandonment of the road-building project, and the land was transformed into Sicily's first nature reserve. Today the Riservo di Zingaro is a haven of solitude, and a walker's paradise.

After your arrival at the parking lot/park office, you may purchase drinks and junk food while changing into hiking boots and enjoying views of the deep blue Mediterranean Sea. Soon you will cross a tiny bridge, traverse a rocky tunnel, and slide effortlessly into a quiet automotiveless world seldom encountered in Italy. The rest of the trail hugs the coast and offers uniformly superb, world-class panoramas of crashing waves, craggy coastline, and formidable pinnacles. Since there are no mechanized means of transport in the reserve, this is one of two walks described in this book which requires a two-way trek. However, the views in both directions are outstanding and ever-changing. You will not be bored. This is also a good opportunity to observe how walking in Italy could be if the government would take the initiative to protect more of this beautiful nation and institutionalize walking as a desirable activity.

While in the area, it is possible to stay in a local hotel, but you may wish to sojourn in fascinating Palermo—seedy port town, lively university center, and capital of Sicily. Take a daytime stroll through the tortuous medieval alleys, stopping to imbibe at cozy

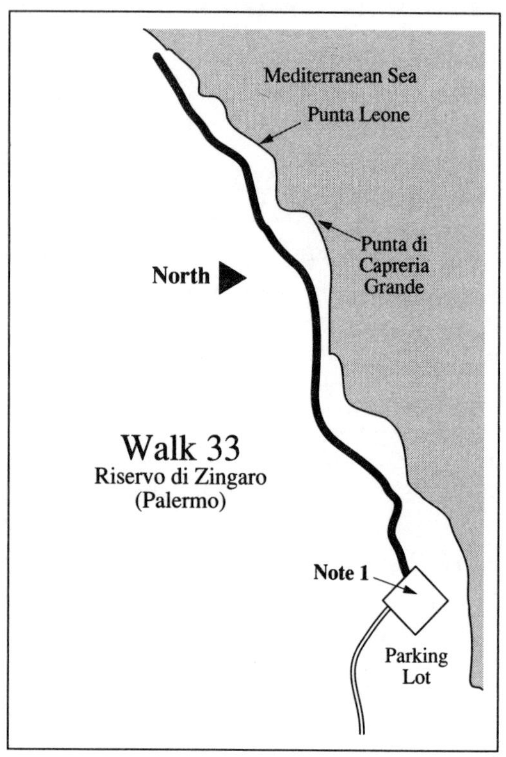

cafes which are snugly arranged about diminutive *piazze*. While wandering about, pay visits to the massive twelfth-century cathedral; the Palace of the Normans, which is currently the seat of the Sicilian parliament; the interesting collection of flora at the Botanical Gardens; a sterling assortment of ancient archaeological discoveries at the Museo Archaeological Regionale; and a variety of lesser churches, palaces, and museums.

Optional Maps: A topographical map indicating park trails is available at the park office in the parking lot.

Time/Distance: 1–2 hours/3–6 miles.

Difficulties: None.

Toilet Facilities: At the parking lot; some privacy.

Refreshments: Refreshment stand at the parking lot.

Getting There: From Palermo take the expressway A19 to Castellamare and then SS187 to Scopello, where there are signs leading to the Riservo.

Trail Notes

__ 1. From the small park office in the parking lot, follow the path that goes though the tunnel you will see above your position at the office. Walk in as far as you wish and walk back out on the same path. There is no public transportation in this protected area.

Suggestions for More Walking

This is a good area for in-and-out walks amidst comely surroundings. The topographical map available from the park office delineates several other walks in the park.

Walk 34: Puglian Coast

Walk: Abbazia San Vito to Polignano sul Mare

70 mins.
3.2 miles (5 km)

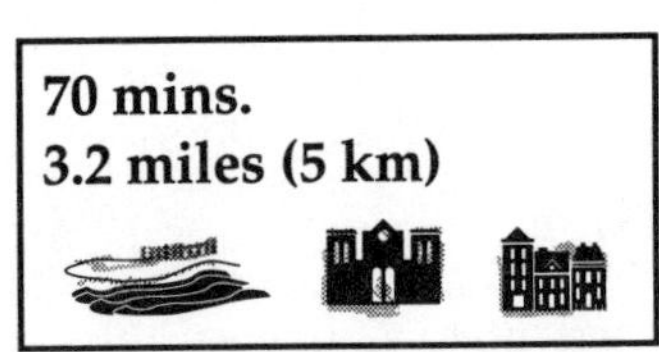

General Description

The Puglian coast lies recumbent for hundreds of miles along the Ionian and Adriatic Seas and forms the heel of the Italian peninsula. The arid, sometimes searing climate invites sunbathing, swimming, and general lethargy; however, when you have had a surfeit of baking and bathing, rouse yourself from somnolent torpidity and trek *con gusto* along a most scenic stretch of meridional seashore.

Today's perambulation begins with a quick bus ride to a narrow, asphalt road leading to the medieval abbey of San Vito. The quick jaunt to the beach along this seldom-used road, lined with olive groves, is quite peaceful and blessed with excellent views of the abbey. Strolling by the abbey, you will soon reach the rocky, sometimes crowded beach where land-hungry, lobster-red humans cling crookedly to large boulders hoping to avoid being washed away in the tide. Continuing along the beach, be sure to take advantage of numerous opportunities to swim and mingle with locals at the beach and at a variety of snack shops. You will also enjoy excellent views of pretty Polignano throughout the walk. The beach eventually joins with the small urbanity of Polignano and the transition from beach to town is quick and intriguing—you will slip down a narrow corridor adjacent to a densely inhabited house and then traverse a small cove to a set of steeply winding stairs for the final climb into town.

In town, you will wander aimlessly about an intricate web of narrow passageways and picturesque *piazze* that comprise Polignano's enchanting medieval quarter. At the cliff-side terminus of this intriguing maze, you will stand rapt in admiration at long views into the deep blue sea. A parting visual sensation can be had from the newer part of town, just north of the medieval section, where you will be captivated by ocular sensations associated with the lovely old town hanging precipitously over the sea.

Optional Maps: None, but it is impossible to become lost.

Time/Distance: 1 hour 10 minutes/3.2 miles (5 kilometers).

Difficulties: A few minutes of walking along a busy road from the bus stop.

Toilet Facilities: Just before you reach the abbey or at refreshment stands; little privacy.

Refreshments: Various refreshment stands along the way; restaurants and cafés in Polignano.

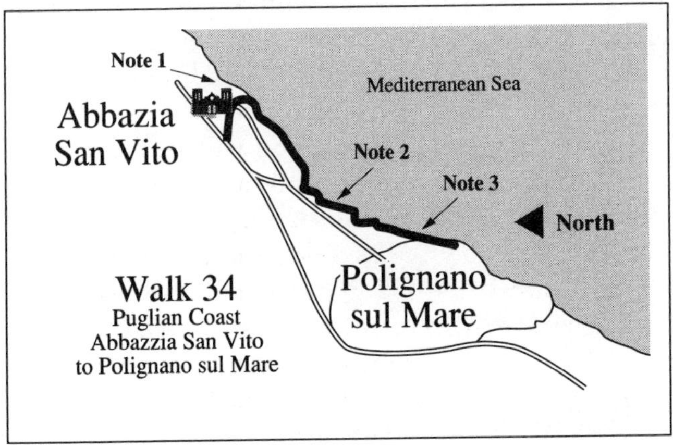

Getting There: From Polignano, take the bus to the road that leads to the Abbazia di San Vito (say to the driver *"alla strada per l'abbazia di San Vito"*). There is no official stop at this road, so you may have to walk back from wherever the driver can stop to where you see the sign indicating "San Vito" where you turn left. The bus is going in the direction of Bari and Mola di Bari. During the summer, there are 2–3 buses per day. Other times of the year there are 5–6 per day. Bus schedules are posted and tickets (you cannot purchase tickets on the bus regardless of what Auto Scuola personnel may say) may be purchased at the Auto Scuola Carone on Piazza Aldo Moro just off Piazza Garibaldi, where the covered bus stop is located.

Trail Notes

__ 1. Walk to the right around the abbey and continue to follow the road for a couple of minutes until you see the first narrow road leading to the beach, where you will turn left and then go right when you reach the beach.

__ 2. About midway through the walk, the beach disappears for a short distance, necessitating a few minutes of ankle-deep water walking.

— 3. Before the final entry into Polignano you will pass down a set of stairs next to a private house and onto a small cove, where you will take another set of stairs up to the other side and arrive in the town.

Suggestions for More Walking

You may double the length of this walk by taking the bus to Cozze, north of San Vito and traversing the coast. It is also possible to walk along the coast from Monopoli to Polignano with a couple of stretches along the road.

Walk: 35: Gargano

70 mins.
3.2 miles (5 km)

***Walk:* Parco Nazionale del Gargano**

General Description

The Gargano promontory, jutting boldly into the Adriatic Sea, forms the spur of the Italian boot and, during the summer, is a beach-lover's utopia. Although increasingly more popular among European tourists, Gargano retains much of its remote charm from the days when it was seldom visited and the main industry was fishing. Today the hotels are frequently packed during July and August, but not far from the most popular strands of sand lie vast stretches of quiet coast and an expansive interior penetrated by few tourists.

Vieste, situated at the tip of the promontory, is the most convenient and congenial base of operations for touring Gargano. Located along a wide sandy beach where warm, deep-blue waves ripple tranquilly over crystalline grains of sand, Vieste defies the chaos and madness that has gripped most of the Italian peninsula. Vieste's main attractions are superb beaches, crystal clear waters, and an eternally shining sun. However, the town itself is quite attractive, especially the whitewashed, maze-like old Arabic quarter where you will enjoy a good wander while gazing into the sea. There is also a small cathedral which is worth a short walk around, and the climb to the castle is rewarded by extensive views of the Gargano coast and the sea.

After about a 30-minute drive south of Vieste, you begin at a lonely, few-car, dirt parking lot which is a harbinger of the preternatural calm that reigns supreme along this most enchanting pathway. Entering this woodsy realm, you will note that initial stretches of the forest have been scorched black by recent flames, producing an eerie, perhaps foreboding landscape as the charred remains of trees stand in stark contrast to the brilliance of the sun and the whiteness of the cliffs. Continuing along the trail past the wilderness burn victims, you will enjoy excellent views of cliffs and sea as you walk high above the Mediterranean. About midway you may wish to pause for lunch at one of the conveniently situated picnic tables. Before arriving at the beach, along a now downward sloping trail, you will pass through a densely forested area where you will enjoy cool shade and lovely glimpses of the shimmering sea through dense stands of dark trees.

Surrounded by steep cliffs and high hills, the sandy beach at Vignanotica is quite alluring. However, even a solitary forest trek in a roadless area does not assure any privacy at such an attractive location. A surprising number of beach potatoes arrive by boat on a daily basis, and a snack bar exists for their culinary pleasure. Relax on the beach, enjoy a good swim, and snack heartily before heading back to the trail.

Optional Maps: Locally available maps of Gargano, but not necessary.

Time/Distance: 1 hour 10 minutes (total time both directions) /3.2 miles (5 kilometers).

Difficulties: About 15 minutes of climbing from Spiaggia Vignanotica.

Toilet Facilities: At the Spiaggia Vignanotica; much privacy.

Refreshments: Refreshment stand at Spiaggia Vignanotica.

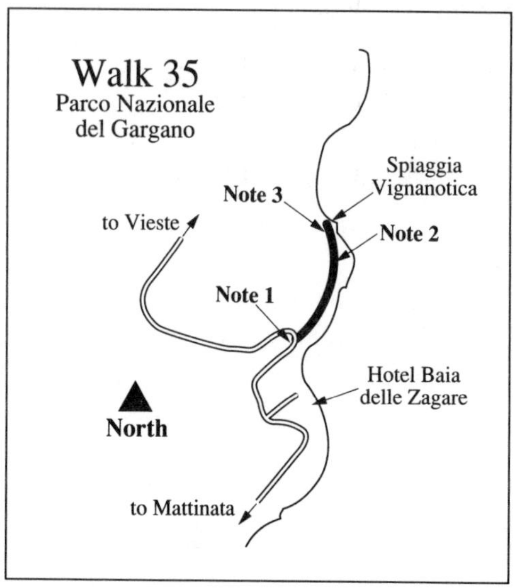

Getting There: The trail is 15 miles (24 km) south of Vieste. If you are coming from Vieste, it is just before you reach the Hotel Baia delle Zagare, which advertises heavily on this stretch of the road. Continue to look to the left as you drive from Vieste; there is a small place to park a couple of cars and there is a large, brown park sign, "Sentiero Pedonale Mergoli Vignanotica," indicating the trail head.

Trail Notes

__ 1. Just follow the trail from where you park the car. There is no other trail in sight.

__ 2. When you come to a fork after about 20 minutes, follow the sign that indicates "Spiaggia Vignanotica."

__ 3. Just before you reach the beach you will have to go under a single strand of barbed wire.

Suggestions for More Walking

Marked trails exist in the Foresta Umbra, which is Gargano's interior high country. The walk to the Foresta Umbra's highest point, Monte Iocatenente, is spectacular but exhausting. Further information is available at the tourist office in Vieste.